STOP HUSTLING GIGS

AND START BUILDING

A BUSINESS

101+ Tricks of the Trade to Help
Entrepreneurs and Self-Employed
People Build a Money-Making Machine

STOP HUSTLING GIGS

AND START BUILDING

A BUSINESS

101+ Tricks of the Trade to Help Entrepreneurs and Self-Employed People Build a Money-Making Machine

by

Joel G. Block, CPA, CSP

ISBN-10: 0-9989341-0-0

ISBN-13: 978-0-9989341-0-5

Printed in the United States.

Production Oversight: Phil Gerbyshak • Phil@PhilGerbyshak.com

Editorial Management: John Peragine • john@johnpwriter.com

Technical Editor: Sarah Sypniewski • sarahsypniewski@gmail.com

Cover Art & Layout: Redbrush • phil@redbrush.com

About the Cover: Successful entrepreneurs, solopreneurs, and self-employed people across all industries radiate momentum, power, energy, movement, action, and force. We are the *red balls*—the ones who put idea into motion; the ones who drive action. As an entrepreneur and leader, I am a red ball, and I expect that you, my reader, are a red ball, too (or at least aspire to be). Study this material well, and become a powerful force in your business and life.

P.S.: When I was a young boy, my grandfather had a Newton's cradle similar to the one on the cover and I spent hours playing with it—wondering how and why it works. This cover reminds me of those wondrous days. Let's all remain curious and continue to ask the hard questions that make us better adults.

TESTIMONIALS

"40 years as a professional speaker and author has shown me that Joel Block is right…most self-employed folks don't think like business builders. Nor do they seem to understand money as well as Joel does. Yes, they have charisma, expertise, and they are articulate. They are usually worth the money they earn. But they don't keep much of it. If you're in business for yourself, read this book twice. Practice this wisdom and become wealthier."

Jim Cathcart, CSP, CPAE
Past President of the National Speakers Association
www.Cathcart.com

"Joel has provided a great overview in simple, easy to understand terms, like how to be 'engaged', rather than 'hired' by clients. He encourages the reader to create systems to make money work harder for all of us.

His knowledge as a hedge fund manager combined with his experience with running his own businesses allows him to address the challenges (and mindset) of entrepreneurs.

Helpful, practical money advice and an honest approach is refreshing as he provides distinctions of how tax impacts each dollar, why continuously putting money aside to invest in revenue-producing assets is critical, and how developing diversified revenue streams is a must for everyone.

You will be challenged when you read this book to look at your business differently, collaborate more with others, and definitely learn how to pay attention to what really matters."

Neen James
Business Motivational Keynote Speaker and Productivity Expert
www.neenjames.com

"*Stop Hustling Gigs and Start Building a Business* is like getting a mini MBA with real-world knowledge and none of the cost. With this book, you will increase your business knowledge and gain the insight you need to succeed. Joel Block has written a straight-talking, no-nonsense guide that will open your eyes to how money works and business runs."

Meridith Elliott Powell
Business Growth Expert & Keynote Speaker
President, MotionFirst
http://www.meridithelliottpowell.com/

"I will never forget the day that I was sitting in a diner in New York City when Joel asked, 'Are you building a business or hustling the next gig?' I nearly fell off my chair. That million-dollar question shifted my mindset in ways that are creating a better quality of life with financial freedom. This incredible book is the culmination of his wisdom that backs up that question by presenting concepts broken down in ways that are more easily understood and more relatable. Don't waste any more time trying to figure out how to be successful in business. Study these 101+ principles and master your financial knowledge!"

Rochelle Rice, CSP, AS
The Movement Expert – Move Your Body. Move Your Mind.
www.RochelleRice.com
NSA Board of Directors 2016-2019

"Just because you have a hobby or skill that you can monetize, that doesn't mean you can build a business that makes a profit and lasts. Joel combines his expertise in business with his investment background to give you practical tips you can use to grow your business and secure your financial future. His no-nonsense insights are there for the taking for anyone with the discipline to put them into action. Don't just buy this book; live it for a year and reap the benefits."

Terry Paulson
PhD, CSP, CPAE

"This is the secret sauce of building a business empire. Joel provides the money strategies, mindset, and management tools you need to build a successful business. He also provides the missing link that the majority of small businesses owners and entrepreneurs don't get: all money is not the same. I believe this book must be in every entrepreneur's library. Buy this book. However, don't just put it on the shelf after you do so; read it, highlight the parts that resonate with you, and then take action. Read it again and again and use it over and over."

Pegine Echevarria, MSW, CSP
2016 Macy's and Minority Business Entrepreneur Magazine *"Woman Who Rocks In Business"*
#3 Fastest Growing Privately Owned Business in North Florida
Inducted into the Motivational Speakers Hall of Fame

"Joel Block knows how to help people generate more income and be more successful. This guide helps both aspiring and current entrepreneurs with business development and process improvement. Joel knows how to build business!"

Commander Mary Kelly, USN (ret),
CEO, Productive Leaders
Author, *15 Ways To Grow Your Business in Every Economy*

"Starting your own business may seem easy, but sustaining profitable success over a long period of time is a whole other thing. Joel Block has provided the formula for long-term success that I wish I had twenty-seven years ago when I started in this business. If you want to profitably run your business and build wealth, you need this book."

Peter B. Stark,
Best Selling Author, Speaker and Consultant
The Only Negotiating Guide You'll Ever Need
www.peterstark.com

"Joel has a brilliant business mind. I interviewed him for *Speaker Magazine*, and the golden nuggets he shared were smart, tangible, and business-changing. He helps entrepreneurs look at money in a different way. I recommend anything by Joel Block!"

Marquesa Pettway
www.TheSpeakerpreneur.com
Speaker Magazine **Columnist**

"When Joel Block speaks, smart people listen. *Stop Hustling Gigs and Start Building a Business* is the book I wish I'd had when I began my speaking career, but I'm grateful that it's here now. The book helps self-employed individuals see our work from a richer, more meaningful perspective. Joel rightly suggests that our goal is ultimately to make a deep, long-lasting, positive impact on the world. This book will help you do just that. Joel Block is a generous human being, a high-character businessperson, and a font of knowledge who every current or aspiring entrepreneur will benefit enormously from."

Bruce Weinstein, Ph.D.
The Ethics Guy®
CEO, The Institute for High-Character Leadership™
Because being ethical is cool—and profitable™

"Joel Block understands the 'money business' and provides a unique insight into thinking about how this relates to your business. The goal is not to be busy, but to be productive and then get your money to work for you for the long term. Whether it is looking at a diverse set of revenue streams, using your resources wisely, moving beyond just providing services or turning your savings into assets, *Stop Hustling Gigs* is the book you want to read."

Jodi Walker, CSP
Chief Creative Catalyst/Owner
Success Alliances
www.JodiWalker.com

"For the past 29 years of speaking and consulting with organizations on 6 continents, I find the biggest issue is that most people spend more time working 'in' the business versus 'on' the business. Working on the business is more strategic and includes figuring out where you need to go to reach your goals, how you are going to fund your efforts, and more importantly—how you are going save the money you will need to fund your desired lifestyle. In this easy-to-read book, Joel gives you ideas on how to look at money and your business in such a way that you will immediately start doing things differently and more importantly achieving better results. This is a must read for all entrepreneurs!"

Ron Karr
Teaching People how to better IMPACT their markets and customers to achieve significant results!
Past President National Speaker Association (2013-2014)
Author, *Lead, Sell or Get Out of the Way*

"It took me over 35 years to learn how to build a profitable business and now Joel Block has captured it all in one book! No fluff, no theories, no guesses – just solid practical ideas that work to build a sustainable business. This is the blueprint you have been looking for to stop working a job and building a business that works!"

Barry Banther CMC, CSP | Senior Partner
Certified Management Consultant (IMC)
Certified Speaking Professional (NSA)
Best-selling author of *A Leaders' Gift - How to Earn the Right to Be Followed*

I dedicate this book to my wonderful wife Sandy—my partner in love and life—as well as to our 3 fabulous kids. It is with all of you in mind that I share this material with readers from every walk of life.

CONTENTS

FOREWORD

Here's the rule for business today—adapt, change, or die. That's it. If you keep doing things the same way you've always done them, someone's going to beat you because they will come up with something better, faster, cheaper, or of greater value. If you don't adapt to change, if that isn't part of your mantra, if you're not looking at continuous improvement—of quality, of market share, of margins, of price or clause and all the inputs that go into the delivering of a product or service—you will fail. Everything in the world around us changes every single day: the seasons, weather, trees, and grass. There's a time for improvement in all things; Darwin taught us that a long time ago, but we seem to have forgotten along the way. If a species can evolve, why can't businesses?

The goal of Joel's book is to help entrepreneurs evolve their businesses. I have been a solopreneur. In fact, I have bought and sold more than 250 businesses, and there are benefits to that way of life. However, to truly find success, you need to grow a business with regular clients, predictable sales, and a dependable cash flow. Don't be tempted to move on before you let your business evolve into a money-making machine.

We're about to go through one of the biggest transformations of wealth we've ever seen—one that will allow entrepreneurs to grow and fund their businesses differently. For a long, long time, we have had to rely on family, friends, or the bank to be able to fund our businesses. But now you can use tools like social media to find other people who can help you achieve your dreams. Self- funding, which is just one of Joel's 101+ business growth mechanisms, is allowing us the opportunity to live the American dream. Joel G. Block is showing us the strategies we all need to build long-term success. And solid businesses are good for each of us and for our economy as a whole.

Jeffrey Hayzlett
Primetime TV & Podcast Host, Chairman C-Suite, and author
of *Network Evolve your Business to Build Long Term Success*

PREFACE

This is a special book with a special agenda that I reveal in just a moment. But before I do that, let me give you the lay of the land.

First of all, ***this book is all about business.*** At its core, this book teaches business thinking for business people in all industries. No matter what your field is, try to think broadly when reading this material in order to absorb and apply it to your life in the best possible way.

Secondly, the material in this book is generally geared towards advanced (meaning more financially successful) professionals because those are the people with existing momentum who can use this material to propel themselves to the next level—but again, all professionals at any level can highly benefit from the tips and tricks in this book. All are welcome here!

This book is made up of ***101+ "tricks of the trade",*** grouped into sections based on the concepts and principles I have used throughout my career for building businesses. Each of these insights is a piece of business wisdom - some of which I use every day. Some insights help me regularly, while some are strategies that I put to use only when I start a new, substantial endeavor, which does not happen too often. Each insight could be a white paper or even a stand-alone book, but the purpose of this collection is simply to create an awareness of the many principles, best practices, methods, mindsets, and tricks of the trade available to you as you build your own "money-making machine". My goal is not to take a deep dive into the details of each element because either alone or through collaboration with others, you will figure it out. That is what resourceful people do.

This material is designed to help you understand why the actions you take are working (or not working) to your satisfaction. If you want to go deeper into any of these insights, get in touch, and we can talk about collaborating to produce more materials.

Warning: Do not try to implement all of these insights at once. Pick a few and work on them first. Then, over time, add a few more. This is not designed to be quick and easy. You are going to have to work on it to gain mastery. But the effort will be worthwhile.

Many people think they understand money, but I am not talking about a high school-level competency of money management and bank reconciliations; I am talking about deeply understanding where money comes from, how money is priced and valued, why people and companies spend or invest it, and what this has to do with getting you paid. This is not a criticism of any kind. It is an invitation into a secret world that few get to visit.

This material includes intermediate techniques for deepening your understanding of business—more specifically, how money works, where it comes from, and how this information matters in how you plan your business and your life. This material is not about economics, and you won't find it in any textbook. It's not complicated, and you don't need special math skills to understand it. It's based in reality and comes from my years of being in a Wall Street business. Almost all of the material is based on my own observations, while some of it is based on great ideas worth sharing that I have learned from other people.

And what *don't* I do here? I don't talk about creating millionaires, or building million-dollar businesses. And except for providing examples when they are helpful to readers, I rarely talk about my personal financial accomplishments, or about how I used to live under a bridge (which I never did) before zooming to financial stardom. I come from middle class roots. I have a basic college education from a public college. But I have street smarts and solid technical training (I started in the CPA business, which is where my initial insights largely come from). The concepts shared here are not gimmicks. It is all stuff and no fluff.

I've been in business for a long time—about 30 years. And for all but the first two years out of college when I worked at Price Waterhouse as a young tax accountant, I have been on my own - always in the deal business. First I was in real estate syndication, then in venture capital, and finally, back to real estate - running the Bullseye Capital Fund. Over the years, some deals have been great. Some, not so much!

Throughout my experiences, I've found specific principles, philosophies, and strategies that have worked for me. Some I learned from great leaders with whom I was fortunate to cross paths. Others are common sense, or perhaps they are well known in business because they are taught in business school or elsewhere. But in most all cases, I put my own spin on them. I have developed my own way of languaging, explaining, or interpreting this material. In true entrepreneurial form, I have made these concepts my own, by looking at them in my own way.

People say nothing is new—and that may be true, but concepts can always be broken down in better, in more easily understood ways. Perhaps how I look at money and business will speak to you as never before. Many people find my simple approach to be more relatable that the usual lingo and industry-speak, and I hope you will find the same.

So you might be wondering what I am selling, and why I wrote a book for entrepreneurs. Or how many entrepreneurs have hired me to help them with their businesses. In the past, I have worked with hundreds of entrepreneurial companies, but more recently, I have stopped doing advisory work in favor of buying, selling, or investing in companies.

While I don't generally sell services to entrepreneurs, I am still very involved in entrepreneurial companies. I advise companies I invest in and I am asked to sit on boards where I can also be helpful. Typically, when I do advisory work, it is only for other hedge fund managers or as an expert for attorneys or a court of law. I like to do the expert witness work because it adds to my credibility in my other businesses.

My motive is that entrepreneurs are some of the finest people I have met in my career, and I want to help them. It pains me to see so many self-employed folks struggle financially even as they do what they love most. They try to keep up the image of an industry superstar who has money flowing in from every direction, but the pain in their faces is real—and obvious.

What will really make the difference to these individuals and anyone reading this book is gaining a new attitude, a new outlook, and a new understanding of money and how business actually works. The methods and mindsets I present here will help you see your business, your future, and your goals much more clearly.

So, then, what is my real special agenda here? This volume exposes some of the wisdom and insights I have accumulated, languaged, and lived for my past three decades in business. In a special way, this material is for my children, so they have a permanent record of how I think and how I see the world. They have seen and heard so much of this material, but I've never shared it with them in such an organized and formal way.

I have collected this material for my kids to better understand how I interpret and then deal with the situations and opportunities that present themselves to me. But you, readers from every walk of life, are also the beneficiaries of that learning and of sharing. As I want my children to benefit from what I have learned about the business and about how people interact in our world, I want you to benefit too.

In general, the richest and most successful people understand money and business in ways most others don't. I want you, my colleagues, to have a similar understanding.

So in a nutshell, why did I write this book? There are 8 primary reasons—and not all are entirely business-driven:

1. I had lots of ideas in my head and I wanted to put them on paper for legacy purposes.
2. In talking to many of my self-employed friends, there seemed to be great interest in understanding these concepts.
3. Those who are self-employed, by their own admission, need business training and many ask for it—but good material that is relevant is hard to come by.

4. My longer-term goal is to create a vertical series—that means continuing to customize the content in this book to meet the needs of CPAs, attorneys, and other specialty groups. This volume for entrepreneurs is just one vertical of many.

5. I always think about sharing, networking, brand-building, and long-term relationship development. A book filled with business and money-making insights can only help with each of these.

6. I want self-employed professionals to understand the importance of "owning things" rather than just providing services. The two are not mutually exclusive.

7. I believe that what goes around comes around and so—in some small way—sharing what I have learned throughout my career is part of my way of "sending the elevator back down," as Kevin Spacey would say.

8. And the goal that would bring me the most joy if I accomplished is: to help others create success. I would love nothing more than for any one of you readers to call me in the near future and tell me that understanding this material helped you make your family more financially secure.

And finally, maybe someday, one of you will call and ask me to help you manage some of the extra money you have been able to accumulate as a result of these insights. If that happens, I will be here for you.

Best of luck and warmest regards,

Joel Block

Joel G. Block
Chief Deal Maker
Bullseye Capital
5737 Kanan Road, Suite 269
Agoura Hills, CA 91301
www.stophustlinggigs.com

INTRODUCTION

I am a Hedge Fund manager (which means investors give me their money to make investments, for which my company receives a share of the profits). As a professional investor and longtime venture capitalist, my long-held belief is that it is hard to make a substantial income and accumulate considerable wealth without a deep understanding of how money and the money business really works. This belief explains my passion for sharing ideas and little known insights on topics that are terribly misunderstood by most people—hence, this book. The fascinating insights I share here provide you with a behind-the-scenes look at the way money moves, and how you can make *yours* move so you can forever change how you price and sell your services. It also forces you to look at your products and services mix, which might help you reconsider what and how much you sell.

I am also a professional speaker. That means I'm an educator who has figured out how to get paid pretty well for teaching. Twice annually, I teach real estate brokers, CPAs, Attorneys, Investment Bankers and others how to set up and manage their own syndication projects or hedge funds. To date, I have provided this training 18 times through three-day intensive seminar programs. This training has spawned over 45 funds and 125 syndications.

We entrepreneurs are positive people. We advise and encourage people to believe that anything is possible. We help people see a better world and what their place in the better world could be. I am a giant fan of this message myself, and I love hearing other entrepreneurs share that message as well. I've got a collection of thousands of memes - all with encouraging and happy thoughts. I love this stuff.

I live my life expecting that opportunities will present themselves. I am open to them. The law of attraction really works: opportunities come to us because we are ready to receive them. But having a million-dollar mindset is only part of the formula; *getting the opportunity* is the next part of the formula. Locking it down and monetizing it is the hard part, and no matter how great your attitude is, the devil is in the details. So what happens when an opportunity shows up?

Most creative-turned-business people see the world in the way that has been taught to them. Many industries generally promote linear thinking rather than leveraged thinking, but we have to ask if this produces optimum results. We have to ask if the results are optimized for today, or if the "playbook" of strategies, plans, and ideas has become tired or out-of-date.

As someone who is in the "money business", I look at situations differently from many other people. My perspective is frequently quite different even from other people who deal with money, such as accountants—partly because they are not actually in the money business.

One of the reasons people in the money business make a lot of money is because we generally think in a geometric manner, whereas so many other people think in a linear fashion. Instead of thinking that one hour equals one unit of pay, consider ways to make that same hour worth five, ten, or fifty times more. Concepts of leverage are very compatible with this kind of thinking.

For starters, self-employed individuals often talk about charging for value instead of time, but there is even more leverage than that to be had, so many people are still leaving a lot on the table. Why not look to experts on money and finance to see how they might address the same issues in a different way? Learn to ask them if there is a geometric solution—or a different and possibly better way to structure the money than how you are doing it. And actually, most business people don't even structure the money at all; they just take what they can get. I'm here to tell you to stop settling!

I have built a successful speaking empire around my primary hedge fund business by teaching others how to get into the same business that I am in. I am known to pull back the curtains on my sales funnel, business models, and other business practices—including sharing the numbers, how I prospect, and even the financial results. Using this information, you can duplicate some of my systems to get similar results.

I am all about adding value. Entrepreneurs must always think about how to add more and more value. Like all successful entrepreneurs, I am a street fighter—doing battle every day in the streets of American enterprise. Using my knowledge, skills, and intuition, I will go toe-to-toe with anyone. Armed with this material and the tools I give you, you will be well prepared to do battle too. Even if you master just a few of these insights, you will begin to accomplish what was previously only a goal. Buckle your seatbelts. Let's go for a ride.

SEEING MONEY THE WAY WALL STREET SEES MONEY

Being in the "money business" means I buy and sell money. I price it and profit from it. If I were in the produce business, I would buy, price, and sell fruit. I do the same with money. Accountants, on the other hand, are in the "keeping track" business. And attorneys are in the law business. Neither is in the money business. Even most stockbrokers are not in the money business; they intermediate and are peripheral to the money business (I can already hear grumblings from stockbrokers who believe they *are* players in the money game—and occupying positions at center court at that!).

So who *is* in the money business? Lenders, bankers, investment bankers, and money managers. In order to be (successful) in this business, we think about money all day long. We tend to think about money in a different way than other people. Now, I have had plenty of people tell me that they understand money, but I am not talking about knowing how to reconcile your checkbook. I am talking about understanding money well enough that you make money from the *money*—not from your time or effort. In this first section, I show you the world and give you insights from the perspective of people who look at and think about money all day long: the Wall Street crowd.

1. Be a Great Street Fighter

Big companies are not necessarily filled with the best that our country has to offer. These big companies don't always get to the top of their industries because they are best in class with the best employees, and it's not because they are lucky either; rather, it's because they have mass and momentum. They have access to more capital and more resources than others—and they have massive economies of scale.

"Wait a second," you might be saying, "why aren't big companies filled with the most awesome talent? Why don't they hire the best people?" The truth is, they do tend to hire the best people, but they have trouble retaining them. A recruiter that I became very good friends with in my youth at Price Waterhouse told me that the firm looks at people in four groups. People in the first group tend to leave the firm over time because they get better offers or to go make their fortunes on their own. Meanwhile, the firm drops anyone in the third and fourth groups right away during the application process—or as soon it becomes obvious where the candidates fall. So who is left? The second quartile. And those are the people who go on to make partner (and who I looked up to like gods when I was 24 years old).

It makes sense, doesn't it? It's not meant to be a slam on corporate or business leaders, but it is an interesting observation—at least in an organization with a definitive pyramid structure as the large accounting firms are.

Then why don't big companies hire little companies if they are so smart? It is because the big companies feel safe with other big companies. There is a kind of insurance in a CYA way. In the late 1980's and early 1990's, technology managers bought IBM computers because if something when wrong, they could point to IBM and say, "we bought IBM, what else could we have done?" This is why big companies and little ones are generally incompatible. However, that doesn't mean it's impossible. I created a business relationship with a Fortune 500 company, but I brought a technology to the table they wanted and could not get anywhere else. So if you are going to try to work with a large company in a material way, be sure that you bring something of significant value to the table to make up for your small size. Remember, little companies innovate and big ones buy our innovations.

To compete, we "little guys" have to rely on our competitive advantage, which are our street smarts and our ability to be great street fighters.

2. Only Want One Client

Seeing this tip, you might think I am an idiot—and that I have probably never taken a class in finance or risk management. You might have a point: having just one client *is* a death sentence. Accountants and bankers call it "concentration," which is the first sign that a business will soon fail. And that is all true, but what if that client is *you*? *I* am my primary client. I am a real estate broker licensed in California for about 30 years, yet I have never taken a listing from any client—but I still generate a lot in real estate fees.

How?

My hedge fund hires my real estate firm to be its real estate broker. My firm also serves as the mortgage broker, investment banker, capital raiser, and more on our transactions. I get paid for each service I render. I don't get grinded or squeezed. There is no fee compression or pressure. And before you run off to check if this is legal, of course it is. But is it proper and ethical? Yes it is, as long as the relationships are disclosed to all participating parties so each investor has the opportunity to approve the relationship in advance.

Now, being self-employed does not necessarily mean you have a *business*. You probably pursue gigs one after the other, and are frequently at the mercy of those hiring you to succeed. In contrast, a business generates money like a machine—over and over. But typically when some hires you, you provide a one-time service. Unless you record a "how-to" workshop that demonstrates your service and then sell it, you are a work for hire.

At some point around 2003, wanted to get into the speaking business. During the first four years after I began my "speaking career", I tried to get hired. I did all of the right things - I had the website, I signed up with speakers bureaus, and I landed exactly…zero gigs.

Out of frustration, I started my own speaking business—a seminar company. I used that company to deliver seminars on how my own business works. I found people who wanted to learn how to be in the venture capital, real estate syndication, or hedge fund business. I had one client who hired me for these engagements: *me*. Because I own the gate for my seminar company, I decide how much I will make, when I will make it, and how much I have to spend to make it happen. Of course, the burden of getting the job done is on my shoulders alone, but I am always willing to bet on me. So your decision is really about whether you are willing to bet on yourself.

Having "me" as a client is pretty cool—and I am a pretty great client. Think about it. My client doesn't whine, moan, or complain. The client doesn't lie, exaggerate, brag, negotiate my fee, or waste my time. He is a great client! Can you construct your arrangements similarly?

3. Avoid Being Hired

Maybe it's just me, but I don't like the word "hire". The concept of "hire me" feels like blue-collar phraseology to me. It is the single most dangerous and limiting phrase for entrepreneurs because it creates a mindset of working for those who hire you—rather than working for yourself. A better phrase I like to use is "engage me". Engaging with clients and prospects is a very positive way to approach your business.

Think about it like this. Every time a client asks for your help—in any capacity—whether for a small job or a long term engagement, they are really asking you to join their team. Think about how flattering that is. This doesn't mean that you have to take a job with the company or association to be part of the team—it's about your contribution to their overall objectives, goals, and outcomes.

Now take this concept and build it into your marketing. Incorporate it into your being. Be someone a company wants on their team. That's a lot different than "hire me".

4. Keep Your Future in Your Own Hands

The alternative to betting on yourself is putting your fate and future into someone else's hands—like an employer. Twenty or thirty years ago, you might have been able to trust that an employer had your best interest in mind and that they would take care of you. These were the years in which pensions were paid for life, providing peace of mind for employees and their families. Much has changed.

Each of us has to take our own temperature on this topic and build our businesses accordingly. Personally, I can't imagine putting the welfare of my family on someone else's shoulders. Partly, it is because of my entrepreneurial nature, but largely, it is about my distrust of the system. Having a job is not more secure than giving yourself a job, because you can be let go at any time. And sometimes when you are let go, you don't see it coming, which can be catastrophic. All of us self-employed people take the responsibility for our own futures very seriously—every day. Not all of us plan for it very well and not all of us know how to maximize our opportunities, but that is what this book is about.

Some self-employed folks are lucky enough to sign large contracts with just a few clients, but is this a safe bet? You put yourself at the mercy of budget cuts and constantly changing personnel, some of who may not want to renew your contract one day. I am not suggesting that you turn down these types of opportunities; rather, think about building a business with multiple streams, as I will describe later so that if you are "fired" or released for any reason, you are not scrambling to rebuild your business. Try not to become too comfortable and let your livelihood and your financial future rest in someone else's hands. And most of all, never put all of your eggs in one basket. And if you think about it, isn't having a job where you work for someone else the same as 100% concentration—or putting all of your eggs in one basket?

5. Be Careful - Entrepreneurship is Dangerous
I recently saw a speaker tell an audience to "be brave for 20 seconds and leap past your fears." That's pretty terrible advice. Without a solid plan, solid strategy, solid business model, and lots of forethought, taking the leap and jumping into action is not a guarantee of anything. He told us how entrepreneurship is a roller coaster, so we need to be brave and ride. However, as best as I could tell, all of the people on the roller coaster on the video he was showing us were wearing harnesses for safety and protection.

Don't count to 20 and jump without the safety and protection of a plan, a funnel, and a well thought-out backup plan.

I am an entrepreneur in my soul. It is my life. I am used to the roller coaster of emotions and financial results. But it's not for everyone. It's certainly not for every spouse. Most in-laws won't understand it, and even your kids may not be able to relate. I'm not telling you to slow down; just be careful, and go in knowing what lies ahead and how much planning and organizing you have to do to be successful.

Keep reading this book to get some real mastery of those plans and business models. So much will become so clear—just be patient and carry on!

6. Don't See All Money as the Same Shade of Green

During a presidential debate in 1992, Ross Perot brilliantly criticized a Clinton staffer who was promoting manufacturing in America and "didn't care whether we make potato chips or computer chips." Perot went on to say, "Anybody that thinks about it cares a great deal…you make more money making computer chips than you do potato chips."

Some activities are more productive than others. Some activities are more profitable. Some activities provide a better return on investment. Some uses of time are better than others. But if you don't understand the underlying mechanics and business issues, how would you know which ones are which?

There is a common misperception that all money is the same shade of green—in other words, that all money is the same. Well, it's not. Some money is better than others. You need to understand the character of the capital in order to make optimal decisions about how you attract and expend the resources you control. In the same way that all manufacturing is not equal, some applications of capital are more intense and innately more profitable. The character of the work service providers perform varies too. Understanding the character of our capital and leveraging this knowledge helps all of us in the entrepreneur world maximize and optimize the potential we each have. I go deeper on this topic in a bit, I promise.

It's funny to me when you ask someone how they are and they respond that they are very busy. I always think to myself (and sometimes blurt out loud) that the goal is not to be busy. The goal is to be productive. Like money is not all the same shade of green, every hour is not the same either—some are better spent than others.

7. Understand the Money

It's hard to make a lot of money if you don't understand the money. Only a small percentage of people can just show up to work and generate money; everybody else has to work to make the money. If you want to be in that first group, you need to have financial literacy - you need to know how money works.

To be successful, you must have an attitude that enables you to optimize your opportunities when they present themselves, but that alone does not prepare you to pounce on and conquer opportunities. Creating success on purpose requires a sense about deal structure and deal-making—and some knowledge of how money works. Self-employed people and entrepreneurs should keep showing and telling people that they can "do it" and that they deserve to be successful, but should also recognize that their good mindset is not enough. Understanding "the money" allows a good attitude to go to work. The best attitude in the world does not put money in the bank. It may open the door to possibilities, but you still have to know what to do when that door opens.

In order to optimize opportunities, you must have a sophisticated understanding of how money works. Begin to consider where money is coming from, and begin to create multiple streams (I talk more about this later in the "Revenue Octopus™" section). The better at this you become, the more money you can generate over the long term. Learn the language of money, and begin applying the right terms and math to it.

8. Build Your Money Machine - and Maintain It

A business is a machine that generates money. This machine does something over and over and churns out money. In a successful business, you don't have to be there to turn the crank; it continues on without you. There are infinite ways to build that machine, but the important issue is being aware of what it is your machine (and company) does. Is it truly a machine, or are you just hustling gigs to churn out money? If you stopped doing those gigs, would you still be generating money? If you want to be a business, then think about your operations as an enterprise instead of as a job that you have given to yourself.

When our kids were small, we would sit around the dinner table, and my wife and I used to ask our three kids questions about the world to find out what they learned in school that day. Sometimes we got the typical child-hood or teenage sassiness, but sometimes we got through to them and the discussions were robust (considering we were talking to children). When our oldest became a senior in high school and began taking an economics course, our conversations became more worldly and business-oriented. We would talk about money, interest rates, supply and demand, and a myriad of other topics. But at the end of the day, I was able to show my kids the "businesses are machines" model. For them, I pointed out that if they wanted money, they needed to build that machine. Dad was not that machine.

Our task at hand is to build the machine, turn the crank to get it started, and keep it oiled and running smoothly. Do you have a business that spits out money, or do you have a job turning the crank on someone else's machine? Spend time thinking about this distinction, as it will impact the amount of money you make, and whether you will ever be able to truly retire.

ON THE CHARACTER OF MONEY

Who cares about the character of money? I do—and you should too.

In this next section, see why the magic is in how you deal with an opportunity. Success is about how you structure terms and negotiate details. It *all* matters—because at the end of the day, what you take home is a result of the details of the deal.

I recently saw a Facebook post that said it is not necessary to know *how*; as long as you find the opportunities, the details will take care of themselves. I can tell you with perfect certainty that whoever wrote that—and all people who promote that type of logic—have a hidden agenda. They may want to believe this flawed logic because they don't *want* to dig into the details, and saying this exonerates them from doing the heavy lifting. But the devil is always in the details—and so is the money.

9. Categorize Your Money

People who don't have a lot of knowledge about money think that all money is the same, but in fact, money has different characteristics. Once you put it into the bank, it may all *feel* the same—it pays the bills the same and it shows up the same. But take a step back, and you will realize that all money is not even remotely the same. Some money is better than others. In an ironic twist, the easiest way to understand this is to look is the way the United States government taxes our money.

Let's say I give you $1,000 for services that you rendered to me. That would be income to you and probably a deduction to me. Alternatively, I could loan you $1,000, and there would be no tax issue for you or me. Or I could give you $1,000 in venture capital investment for injection into your business to help you grow your company with no tax consequence still—but the catch is that venture money is not a loan. Rather, it creates ownership for me in the business.

Alternatively, you could make a sale for $1,000. The $1,000 sale would be taxable, while the venture capital investment would not be taxed. So even though in all cases, you receive the exact same amount of money, and they look the same on the bank statement because they both show up as $1,000 in your account, in fact, the characterization of these transactions is entirely different.

People in the money business organize the different types of money that come into a business in a way that optimizes everything about the capital structure. It's easy to see on a tax return how this works, and although we don't want to get deep into the weeds on how the accounting treatment works for various types of income, understanding these concepts is pretty important. Tax planning is all about making sure that the different buckets (or money with the same characteristics) that you have flowing through your tax return on an annual basis, is optimized.

For example, if you have a lot of capital gains, then you might want to recognize some capital losses to neutralize the effect of the gains. If you have a lot of long-term capital gains, you would want to offset those against long-term capital losses. Or if you have a lot of long-term capital losses, you especially want to optimize those because it can only be deducted in small increments. You don't have to become an expert in the details; just understand the concept that money has various definable characteristics.

Then by understanding the buckets, you can strategize and optimize your revenue streams. You must embrace this concept, or your business planning efforts may fall short of your goals.

How you classify and organize your money matters. It drives how you create your business plan. By way of a different example, one of my colleagues has a robust practice of recruiting and placing the most senior attorneys at some of the biggest and most prestigious law firms. His compensation is a percentage of the first year compensation that the client receives. Since a senior attorney's compensation can be $1,000,000 or more, this recruiter can make pretty big money. But what if the law firm that hires the attorney characterizes $500,000 as salary and the rest as an allocation for business expenses, such as funding the attorney's home office and a host of other creative expenses? Since the recruiter only gets paid on "first year salary", do you think the recruiter will care how the "hirer" categorizes the money? You bet. My friend tells me that this has actually happened to him before.

10. Make It All About Assets

Many small business owners and those who are self-employed have a hard time understanding the concept of working for money and how that differs from owning assets. Ownership has its privileges. Make it your goal to own revenue-producing assets.

When you own things, you can sell them later. But make sure the things you own are appreciating assets. Rent or lease depreciating ones. Consider your car. It is a depreciating asset; it loses value over time. Unless you plan on keeping the car for a long time (like seven years or more), it is not an asset you want to own, because as you keep paying, you quickly end up owing more than the car is worth. Consider renting or leasing a car instead. There are all kinds of assets you can own that pay you dividends over time. Own rental property. Own investment assets. Make your money work for you so that someday you won't have to work for money.

Note: this is not an either/or type of situation. It is more of a hybrid concept. Try to own assets in your area of work, so that eventually, you have something you can sell.

For example, suppose Bill works at a restaurant that he owns. He makes money for his time working from the salary he pays himself, but he also owns the profit after expenses, plus there is a built-in asset he can sell one day. You have to begin thinking in a different way. You have to decide if are you just hustling gigs, or if you are building a business.

11. Take Your Revenue From Assets

From a taxation point of view, the most expensive revenue is personal services revenue, and guess which kind of revenue most self-employed people make? Yep—personal services revenue (because you are personally generating the revenue from your own services). There are not many tax breaks on this kind of revenue, and in fact, it can be taxed extra as self-employment income to make up for the FICA (Social Security) tax that you are not paying through a paycheck.

It's easy to understand the character of cash when you think about how it is taxed. To explain it, I'll show you the tax effect on several different transactions I conduct:

> Selling a keynote (or any services for that matter)

> Selling books, tapes, magazines, or souvenirs

> Securing a book contact

> Flipping a piece of real estate

> Selling a long-held piece of real estate

Here is the impact of five separate transactions:

Revenue Generating Activity	Box	Maximum Income Tax Rate	Sales Tax	Social Security Tax	Sale Amount	Income Tax Due	Sales Tax Due	Social Security Tax Due	Total Taxes	Net for You	Effective Tax Rate
Sell a keynote.	1	39.6%	0%	15.4%	$10,000	3960	0	1540	5500	$4,500	55.0%
Sell your books tapes and souvenirs.	2	39.6%	8%	0%	$10,000	3960	800	0	4760	$5,240	47.6%
Secure a book contact.	3	39.6%	0%	0%	$10,000	3960	0	0	3960	$6,040	39.6%
Flip a piece of real estate.	4	39.6%	0%	0%	$10,000	3960	0	0	3960	$6,040	39.6%
Sell a long held piece of real estate.	4	20.0%	0%	0%	$10,000	2000	0	0	2000	$8,000	20.0%

I can bring in more revenue if I shift from just making money on gigs and products to making some capital gains on something like real estate because the effective tax rate is so much lower. Not many entrepreneurs can do it right away in their business, but it's something to think about when growing wealth and producing your money-making machine. You have to begin putting money aside. Do whatever gigs you need to do to generate income, but begin to push your savings into assets.

12. Categorize Your Revenues

The following table demonstrates a simple way to categorize revenues. To make more money in your business, you should have a mix of these, but again—over time, you should push your money into Box 4 to get the money to work for you. Shouldn't your money be working as hard for you as you do for it?

Table of Revenue Categories

BOX 1	BOX 2
Revenues from rendering personal services (hourly and salaried work—you have to show up and spend time in order to be paid). This is trading time for money, and is the weakest way to generate money—but it's far and away the most common. Even though the numbers can be large, service provider money falls into this category. You generally have to show up to get paid.	Transactional or value-add revenue is made one time, such as a commission or other type of fee. This is somewhat tied to the amount of effort (hours spent). You do have to do something to earn this money, so you are still trading time for dollars, but it's potentially on a value-driven basis, which creates a higher yield than an hourly rate.
BOX 3	**BOX 4**
Recurring revenue is a stream of revenue that you get from selling something that is going to produce revenues over time (e.g., web site memberships, subscriptions to newsletters). It takes some time to build the revenue stream, but produces a very high yield because the time required to maintain is very small. These are royalty streams. You are not constantly selling these items, but they continue generating income over time.	Passive or asset-based revenue is generated without any physical effort or time commitment from the owner (e.g., rents from an apartment building—the building produces the rents). Money that is produced on capital has an infinite yield on time, so it is measured on capital to make comparisons relevant. This is how all really wealthy people make money.

13. Build Your Revenue Octopus™

It is imperative for a small, rapidly growing business to have a diverse set of revenue streams. I call this diversification a "Revenue Octopus™". The Revenue Octopus™ says that a rapidly growing business, in order to create or sustain hyper-growth, has to have approximately eight different revenue streams (or tentacles). Now this does not mean that a business will be in eight different businesses at the same time. It is really about identifying a revenue stream and then repurposing that revenue stream into another marketplace, adapting the product, or repackaging or remerchandising it so that more money can be made the second time the product is sold than was made the first time that the product was sold.

The Revenue Octopus™ is much bigger than the concept of brand extension. The Revenue Octopus™ means going deep with customers, which means that it costs a great amount to get a customer to spend the first dollar. It costs less to get that same customer to spend a second, third, or fourth dollar with you. When you create a Revenue Octopus™ that is derivative of the same customers or the same concepts, you can begin to see and then harness the power of a Revenue Octopus™.

For example, I had a media company client before they were able to secure a solid injection of capital from an investor. With the goal of getting them some capital, in the strategic planning phase of our relationship, we created a Revenue Octopus™ for their new television network. The network generated revenue from subscriber fees that were paid to it by cable operators. It often ended up being zero to very little, so we needed more ways to generate revenue. We brainstormed the many other places where revenue could come from, such as:

> Advertising
> Internet, including digital advertising and video on demand
> Syndication rights: once content was produced, other networks could buy it from them to fill time on their networks

These are just a few, but we came up with many other revenue streams that they were able to add to the network over time.

When a company is dependent on a single revenue stream for all of its revenue or all of its selling, it could find itself in a compromised situation, should that revenue stream ever diminish.

Starbucks has a great Revenue Octopus™. They have added the sale of music in their coffeehouses. Customers come in for one activity (to drink coffee), but they end up with another consumption opportunity, which is buying music. Offering music sales provides a better experience for the customer, which is part of the show. Another part of Starbucks' masterful Revenue Octopus™ includes selling coffee beans in bulk in places like Costco, as well as packaging Frappuccino and other drinks and selling them in supermarkets across the world. Their success in creating revenue streams goes on and on.

As a service-provider, you can consider the following different revenue streams to help build a comprehensive Revenue Octopus™. In addition to your service fees, consider which of the following you could add to your menu of products and services:

> Publishing services
> Commissions or success fees
> Expert witness services
> Mentoring and coaching (to individuals)
> Consulting and advisory services (to business)
> Telephone and web seminars
> Subscription newsletters
> Sales of books, workbooks, and products
> Sales of advertising and sponsorships
> Seminars, trainings, and workshops
> Assessments & Membership programs

The diversification of a Revenue Octopus™ offers self-employed people so many different ways to generate revenue and profits, but keep in mind that the tentacles are not all created equal and they have different yields; some activities do a better job of producing immediate cash flow. Typically, personal services do the best in generating funds immediately, but they generally have lower yields and don't create much long-term residual value.

On the other hand, some tentacles produce great long-range value, but they take great planning, execution, and lots of time to develop. These are typically the ones with the highest yields and real enterprise value someone might buy from you.

You can mix and match short-term goals with longer term goals so your business accomplishes what you want it to do. Each tentacle will have its own financial character. Some business models and delivery mechanisms create enterprise value, while others are only about cash flow. By combining different types of revenue streams, you can create a rocket booster effect on your overall income and company value.

14. Spread Out Startup Costs

When an auto manufacturer decides to build a new car, there are a number of expenses they must consider. They must hire engineers, build factories, and buy the equipment needed to build the car. When tallied, the upfront expenses could be $5 billion to roll the first car off the assembly line. Once that is accomplished, they do not need to duplicate the process of creating the design or equipping a factory, so the next car the rolls off the assembly line for a much smaller number, such as $10,000. That amount is just to pay for the incremental cost for materials and labor to produce the next vehicle. The more cars they produce, the less it costs to produce per unit because they divide the up-front costs by more vehicles. Thus, spreading those costs out over more units is good for the manufacturer.

No matter what business you have, there are some start-up costs. That is why we call it capitalism. Business requires some amount of capital—money—to get started. Luckily for most small business owners, it does not take $5 billion to get started, but there is some capital needed to get the business rolling. For example, you probably need to advance the following, and more:

> Website
> Clothes

> Travel funds

> Video

> Coaches and trainers to enhance your skills

> Conferences and networking opportunities

> General working capital—for other requirements

> Extra reserves—just because you never know

Your first gig, like the first car, requires those start-up costs in order for you to produce it. Of course, you cannot bill your first client all of what you have invested, but it is a concept to think about. The more jobs you do over time, the less each will cost to produce, which increases your net income over time. Remember, you have to think about money differently. The amount printed on the check is different than the money that you actually get to keep for yourself after you factor in the expenses of producing and selling the gig.

Many people who are self-employed have limited resources, especially when they are starting out. Therefore, they must be extra careful and use them wisely. If they use up all of their funds on attending a seminar and have nothing left to have their website done professionally, it can have a negative effect on their business. There has to be a balance.

15. Invest in Yourself, Invest in Your Business

After the initial investment in your company, you need to "sharpen the saw," as Stephen Covey suggests. You need to be willing to continue to invest in more education, fees for associations, better websites, and even updated headshots (who are we trying to fool with those photos from 10 years ago?).

You must make the concerted effort to put your money back into your business in these and other ways. This means that you can begin to buy assets, but you must set aside the money and be consistent about it. Once you understand the nature of money, it will become clearer which shade of green your money is—meaning, which money and assets are most important for the long run.

A trap many entrepreneurs fall into is that instead of putting money back into their company as future capital, they upgrade their lifestyles. They may have been making $80K a year, but are living at a $100k a year lifestyle. The rationalization goes, "if only I could make that extra $20k, I would be able to make ends meet. If I make $30K more, I can begin to invest in retirement or other necessities."

The reality is that if we begin making $110k a year, we begin living at a $150k lifestyle. It happens at all parts of the income spectrum. Lots of people who make $1 million live at the $1.1 million level. For many people, no matter how much they make, it's just not enough. You have to make whatever you make be enough. Make a plan for investing in yourself and your business, and you will be able to grow it over time.

16. Focus on Yield - Not on Your Hourly Rate

Many people think about revenue in terms of their hourly rate. When booking upcoming gigs and jobs, you might charge a certain number of dollars per hour, but have no guarantee of what the final invoice will actually be. But in looking at a previous job, you know what your fee was, so it's a fixed amount. Looking backwards, you have more information about what really happened. With the benefit of hindsight, you know how many hours you worked, how many dollars you made, and how much money it took to get you those dollars. If you divide the total you actually made for the project by the total hours you actually invested in the project, the results is the average hourly rate for that project. That average hourly amount is what I call "yield".

A speaker colleague recently told me he makes $10,000 for a one-hour speech, so the hourly rate is $10,000. I immediately called bull and after adding up the preparation time, including client interview, selling time, contract administration, travel in both directions, and ancillary activities, he can count over 50 hours - so the hourly rate (yield) was under $200 ($10,000 divided by something over 50 hours). I don't have an opinion on whether this is a lot or a little—or on whether it is good or bad. You don't have to justify your yield to me or anyone else—but you owe it to yourself to justify it to yourself. If you don't fully understand what is going on in your organization, how can you make changes and improve?

17. Prioritize Your Spending

Everyone has exactly enough money for the things that matter to them. My wife and I once invited some friends to go to Disneyland with us and all of our kids. They declined because they were a little short on money. But two weeks later, they went to Knott's Berry Farm. Clearly, it wasn't the money—they just preferred to go to Knott's Berry Farm. The lesson here is: if your prospects are not saying yes to you, you just might not be hitting the right priority for them—because they always have the money. The question is whether they want to give it to you or not.

And on the flip side, you have to give thought to your own spending. Owning a business requires planning. Each of us needs a roadmap to get to the destination (goal) that we have set. Entrepreneurs need to spend the time to develop goals and objectives, and then create a business plan around them—otherwise; they might run into prioritization problems later. For example, sometimes, we must prioritize our spending to make sure we're spending money on what matters most to our business growth, rather than what we want at the moment.

18. Build a Business Someone Can Buy

Many people would prefer to pull money out of their businesses rather than squirreling revenue and assets away to create a something sellable in the future when they are ready to retire or move on. This is a mistake. You should aim to build a valuable business that a buyer will want down the road. This means you cannot treat your business and revenue streams like a piggy bank.

Let's say you work in different places, and you often take your spouse to make mini-vacations out of it. This sounds great for some people, but that is called a "lifestyle business". Lifestyle businesses are generally worthless to a buyer. It is not something you can put a price tag on and sell. You must have assets or revenue streams for someone to buy (client lists are not generally valuable assets unless they stay with the buyer, which is typically unusual).

To be clear, there is nothing wrong with a lifestyle business, but many successful entrepreneurs who are able to actually sell their companies go on to use the money to fund their retirements. If you don't have anything to sell after you have worked for your lifetime, you will have to make other arrangements to fund your lifestyle if you slow down or stop working altogether. Something to think about.

19. Know Your Business' EBITDA

What is EBITDA and why is it important? EBITDA stands for "Earnings Before Interest, Taxes, Depreciation, and Amortization". This is a mechanism for determining the numerical or monetary value of a company by putting a variety of different companies onto a similar and comparable platform. In other words, it enables companies to be evaluated on an apples-to-apples basis.

Investment bankers and buyers of companies use the EBITDA formula so that they can value companies for purchase and for sale. It helps them know what to make in a down payment and approximately how much that business will cost to run. Many companies sell for three to seven times their EBITDA factor, though it could be much more or somewhat less. So if a company has an EBITDA of $1 million, it might be worth $3 to $7 million on the open market. Small companies are valued this way, while larger public companies are valued somewhat differently.

EBITDA is generally considered the real earnings of a company and a good predictor of cash flow for a buyer. Most lifestyle businesses have a very low EBITDA because owners, in the interest of minimizing taxes, expense many items the IRS might question, such as non-business use of cars, gasoline, meals, travel, home office space, and more. When trying to sell, owners frequently try to "add back" these non-business expenses to increase EBITDA and therefore get a larger multiple on the company's earnings if there is to be a sale. Recasting operating income is not easy to do—and it may not be plausible, which is why some company owners begin to reduce deductions in the 2 or 3 years before a planned sale.

HARD QUESTIONS

Some questions are so uncomfortable that as business people, we avoid them like the plague. But *always* ask the hard questions—of yourself and others. Here are a few good ones I ask regularly.

20. How Badly Do They Need Me?

Contrary to popular belief, your value is irrelevant—by itself. After all, few things matter in a vacuum. To really understand your value, you must know how much the prospect or client needs you. If you render a commodity service, like accounting or legal counsel, then it's pretty easy to figure out what your value is—just compare it to others in your industry. For many other self-employed folks, it is not quite as easy, and that is good news. But how much you are worth to others depends a lot on the kinds of problems you solve and how badly the prospect or client needs that type of problem to go away. For professional salespeople, prospects with problems are easy to spot. Good sellers are like sharks, hunting their prey. Sharks can smell blood a mile away. Can you?

It is well known that in business, *there are no problems—only expenses.* Every business problem can be made to go away if the right resources are expended to take care of it. When a company or organization has such a problem, and you are the solution, you must understand the problem and your specific ability to solve the problem for the client before putting a price tag on it. Of course, more serious problems yield bigger paydays.

The real determinant of your value is your ability to sell. In my core industry, deal promoters ask me what the right amount is to pay the investors.

The answer is always the same: "it depends on how good of a seller you are." If you are a strong seller, pay less. If you are a weak seller, pay more. In my world, everyone understands this. This is true for pretty much any industry. Regardless of your intrinsic value, the better seller you are, the more you will be able to sell your services for. So don't stop working on your selling skills.

Bottom line: the more they need you, the more they will pay. The easier you are to replace, the less they will pay. Figure out what—specifically—clients need from you so you can maximize your value. This is an example of how money follows expertise, but I'll get to that later.

21. What Is the Hidden Agenda?

I recently responded to a Facebook post where someone was looking for advice on ways to increase his yield on some investment. I suggested putting some assets into a Self-Directed Individual Retirement Account. This suggestion was met with great fury by someone suggesting that, according to a certain study, when individuals self-direct their assets, they make less than when being guided by the caring hand of a trained and licensed professional. Sensing lots of hidden agenda, I looked the guy up and sure enough, he was a stock broker-type who makes no fees when people self-direct their own assets. I disengaged from the discussion because I won't argue with people that have a hidden agenda. Always be on the lookout. There are a lot of hidden agendas out there, especially in our world of relentless hype and self-promotion.

22. How Hard Is It?

This is the flip side of "money follows expertise". I would not try brain surgery, but it is amazing how many surgeons have told me how easy real estate investing looks and how anyone can do it. The truth is so much more complicated than that.

Everything is hard until you learn how to do it. Some things are simple to learn, while others may take a lifetime to grasp. What's important to remember is that you should never underestimate the difficulty of learning a new task. When you do this, you let your guard down. The only times I have been smacked in the face is when I've let my guard down, like when I've overestimated the simplicity of a task or underestimated the skills of my competitors. Or worse, I might have overvalued my own capabilities.

Some professions seem easy to learn and get into, but once people try it out and spend a lot of time and money on it, they find that it's a lot harder than they thought. Acquiring the actual skills of a new profession is hard, but making money at it is an even harder task—yet people leap from their full-time jobs with self-generated delusions. Spend the time, ask questions of the professionals already active in the field, and be prepared to work hard. Everything is harder than it looks. And as an added bonus, if you expect it to be hard, you may find it to be a little easier than you think.

23. How Well Do I Know My Business?
Do Realtors understand real estate? If they really understood it, why would they sell any good parcels to you? Or maybe they do understand it, and they just keep the best properties for themselves, leaving you with the scraps. You have to wonder. But like everything else in life, a "best property" is not black or white. It is subjective for every buyer.

For example, on a scale of one to ten, my fund brokers properties that we grade as six and below; we only build syndicated investments around the better properties. But just because a property is a six to us does not mean that it is not an eight to someone else with different criteria. We only deal with other professional investors and like to turn properties over quickly, whereas some people like to hold them for five years or more. There are lots of reasons why we might not like something that is perfect for someone else, and we know those reasons inside and out.

For the record, I am not bashing Realtors. We deal with dozens of very high quality brokers all over the country. I just want to point out how important it is to be really clear who the experts are when you hire them—just like you must be an expert for people to want to engage with you.

Bottom line: we know what we are doing and we execute according to our plan. How well do you know what you are doing? Are you able to put your finger on the right clients, the right prospects, the right leads? Are you able to separate the winners from the time wasters?

The better you know your subject matter and the better you know your audience, the more likely you are to connect the dots between the two and start making money.

24. Who Really Knows Money?

CPAs, attorneys, and financial advisors look at money through a window. They don't roll the dice with their own money and they don't take risk. Investment bankers and asset managers know money because they likely have a vested interest in it if they invest their own money. Their compensation depends on their understanding of it—and on successfully making money move.

The money business is a Wall Street business—it's a risk business. Some people outside of it may know the money business, but I haven't generally come across many of them. Be careful about taking advice from people who are not at risk in a transaction. That includes being careful about taking the advice of consultants and advisors who have a different stake in the outcome than you do. And keep this in mind when you are selling your services to a buyer who might be wondering about your stake in the deal if they engage with you. I once heard Mark Cuban say something that really resonated with me: "never take advice from someone who doesn't have to live with the consequences." To me, that about sums it up. You should look at people that way, and remember that they also look at you that way—so be prepared to answer the hard question about your participation and longevity. More specifically, be prepared to explain which side of the table you are on.

25. What's the Hard Part?

Consider the advice of Steve Martin from his 1970's routine: "if you want to be a millionaire, the first thing you do is get a million dollars." Oh right!

Sure! Why didn't I think of that? When something sounds too easy or too good to be true, well…then it probably is. Product promoters can say that they have the secret to wealth in five easy steps, but if it were that easy, everyone would be doing it, and then nobody would be making money at it.

I also wonder: if they have the secret, and the secret is so lucrative, why aren't they just doing the business they are promoting instead of teaching others to do it? Maybe they have a hidden agenda. Or maybe they are being less than truthful.

Whatever the reasoning behind it, the hard steps are almost always left out—on purpose. You have to always ask yourself, "what steps are people leaving out? What's the hard part?" No one ever tells you the hard part, because you would not buy what people are trying to sell you. Building a nuclear bomb is not as hard as you might think. The hard part is finding the uranium to make it go boom. Getting in front of people and delivering a speech is not the hard part. Fixing a leaky faucet is not the hard part. Getting hired and getting paid for it is the hard part.

In fact, so few people are willing to do the hard part that if you just focus on getting good at the hard part, you would not be able to handle all of the business and success that would come your way. First, identify the hard part. Then, focus on the hard part. Get great at it, and watch the trajectory of your career explode!

THE BUSINESS OF BUSINESS

You run a business, perhaps much to your chagrin. The prevailing attitude among many self-employed folks seems to be that "this business would be more fun if we didn't have to do the business part." That means that the best *sellers*—not necessarily the best service providers—are going home as the winners. Of course, if you aren't good at the craft itself, then you should probably sell someone else's services instead of your own. Either way, a successful entrepreneur has to have strong sales skills and a robust business component to their effort.

26. Set Up a Solid Business Structure

You might not think this is relevant to you because you might be contracted as a sole proprietor. If you hold onto this image for yourself - guess what? You will always be a one-person show without the ability to scale or create a financial future for yourself, as you will always be working.

When the time comes, you will need to hire a CPA and/or a lawyer to set up a business structure. Setting up the correct type of entity to begin with can save you a lot of money and headache in the long run.

Always check with your attorney and/or accountant for specific advice that applies to your unique situation. Understand that corporate and LLC structures are not all they are cracked up to be. They are expensive to set up and maintain. Work carefully with your CPA and attorney to determine what you really need. Maybe a proprietorship with some good liability insurance will suffice.

27. Document Your Partnerships

If you choose to work in partnership with other people—which I think is great—document your agreement on paper. Set up some controls to make sure everyone does what they say they are going to do, and include an "ejection button" in case they don't.

When you have active partners, the agreement can be rather simple, but having even one single passive partner necessitates much more complicated and costly documentation. Taking in capital from passive partners is an advanced technique, so be careful! It might be over the head of your neighborhood attorney (because it thrusts the transaction from business law into securities law), so ask about that. But all partners, whether passive or active, should have a proper partnership agreement or Operating Agreement prepared by a licensed attorney.

As an aside, my very dear lawyer friend Larry Rothstein wrote an article that I posted on my blog in 2011 called "I've Never Litigated Over a Good Contract". You are welcome to search for it there. If that doesn't give you a hint about the value of hiring a good attorney, I can't be any more direct.

28. Stay Fresh to Keep Good Margins and Multipliers

Margins in mature companies get very small, so making money requires lots of volume. In early stage companies, margins (and stock price multipliers) tend to be very high because these companies cannot do large volume, but they have tremendous potential. Plus, new companies, new technologies, and new ideas have more potential and value than mature ones that have already been depleted of much of their potential value.

As we entrepreneurs mature, we must reinvent ourselves, or risk becoming stale. We must come up with fresh and new material. A new skill. A new offering. A book. Without an injection of new ideas, the value of an entrepreneur will decrease and so will what they are trying to sell. Isn't the goal to increase your fees over time, and not lower them? Part of the answer is to stay fresh and continue to bring new ideas to bear. This is a great way to keep your fees and margins high.

29. Don't Rely on the Fantasy of Financial Projections

When looking at financial statements, remember: even if something is printed on paper, that doesn't make it automatically accurate or true. If you are reviewing something that is very important and numbers are involved—especially numbers that represent balances in cash or other accounts—ask for underlying documents, such as bank statements, to corroborate or verify that what is being purported is actually true.

More significantly, when someone provides with you with a projection of potential future financial activity, be especially suspicious. Although I don't do them anymore, I have prepared thousands of financial projections in the past, and I know what kind of game-playing goes on. In fact, I usually caution readers of financial projections to be careful by telling them that when I was working at Price Waterhouse, I got so good at doing projections, even I believed them!

30. Fixed vs. Variable Costs

These next two sections are important. I start with a brief vocabulary lesson, but don't let it turn you off. I'm teaching you about money going out because it is important to know what the different types of costs are so you can plan and budget. I also want you to understand how your clients plan and budget for the expense of bringing you in to provide services.

A *fixed cost* is an expense that probably reoccurs and is consistent and predictable. These are items like your rent and payroll. It could also include an auto lease, equipment lease, or anything subject to a contract. You probably can't reorganize out of these types of expenses. These costs are also known as overhead.

A *variable cost* is one that is not predictable and may be temporary in nature or is dependent on a level of activity. Hiring a company to build your website is an example of a variable cost. When the project goes away, the cost ends.

When considering how your clients budget for you, consider that a one-time gig is a variable cost for the organization hiring you, whereas a year-long contract is fixed, planned for, and budgeted. This is why many self-employed people find they are constantly hustling for gigs. Variable costs are controllable by the company spending the money. A business can decide or control when they want to pay for a variable cost and set a budget for it. On the other hand, a business cannot easily control fixed costs.

When you're self-employed, it's important to understand variable costs because spending funds on something like a consultation or talk is a variable and discretionary expense for companies or organizations, and they want to control what it will cost them. Organizations develop a budget and they try to stay within it. Remember this, because *they* are in control of that budget and how much they "want" to invest. But budgets are not fixed—and the amount in each line item is not necessarily locked in.

When I tip in a restaurant, the restaurant passes along what would otherwise be a fixed expense for the restaurant to me, the patron. By converting some of its payroll into a charge that consumers bear, the restaurant industry saves a tremendous amount of money. What fixed costs can you convert into a billable expense and pass along to your clients?

Money can always be moved around—if somebody wants to move it bad enough.

31. Direct vs. Indirect Expenses

A *direct expense* is one that occurs directly "because of" a particular event. If you are hired to perform a service—let's say give a training—and you have to pay for a flight and a hotel room to get to the client, these are direct expenses. You would not have to pay these if not for the booked job.

Indirect expenses are items you buy because you want them or need them, but not because of a particular client or activity. These are costs of doing business. Indirect expenses are frequently fixed costs in that they are part of the overhead of your company. Examples of indirect expenses are your computers, cell phones, or tablets. Automobiles and other equipment are also indirect expenses.

My goal is to have as many direct expenses as possible in order to have the option to charge them back to clients. This is critical when you are negotiating contracts because you want to be sure you are charging your direct costs of travel and time and not just rolling them into your fee. Your fee is compensation for the services provided for them. Remember, that is a variable cost for them. Your expenses are separate from that and need to be billed as a direct expense over and beyond your fee. Some clients prefer to receive one invoice for everything; they like the fee to be inclusive of travel, lodging, meals, and incidentals. As long as you understand the concept of collecting your fee and your direct expenses, you can bill for them any way you want.

32. Know the Super Top Line

Most people understand the concept of top line and bottom line. Your top line represents your income (also called "gross revenue") and your bottom line (also called "net income") represents what is left over for you after deducting your expenses. There is a third line not everyone has heard of or understands, and that is the *super top line.*

The super top line is the aggregate amount of all the business a company does, but it does not only represent the money that belongs to the company. This is important because you might hear someone state how much they did in business last year, and that number might sound huge, but it could be a super top line number, not a top line.

Here's an example. Suppose a speakers bureau sells speakers to events, and the total of all business from all speakers for the year adds up to $6 million in total business. That is their super top line. The bureau might make 25% of that amount as their fee, so their top line (gross revenue) is only $1.5 million dollars. After all of their expenses ($1.2 million), their bottom line (net income) is $300,000. So when a representative says they did $6 million in business, you should figure out whether that is their top or super top line number. It puts things in perspective and makes one business or situation comparable to another.

To be fair, some people think it is okay to include the gross speaker revenue in the bureau's top line revenue and then subtract 75% as a "cost of goods sold" before subtracting the bureau's business expenses to arrive at the bureau's net income. Likewise, advertising agencies can book $500 million in ads for clients and include that in their top line revenue before deducting 85% cost of goods sold (i.e. retaining 15% commission), or mortgage companies can include hundreds of millions of loans and subtract 99%, leaving just the one point they typically receive as compensation.

How you describe your business depends on how you want others to perceive you. If your state has a gross revenue tax, you will probably only count the money that belongs to you—which is the top line—but if it doesn't, you may use the super top line because it makes your business look bigger than it really is. Depending on how you keep your books, the bottom line should be the same, but the apparent size of the company can vary dramatically.

33. Don't Let the Numbers Lie to You

Not everything is as advertised; people can shift numbers all different ways. Someone might manipulate numbers to say they did $1 million in business this year. What may be the reality is that they signed a five-year contract that equals $1 million, but really, they made $200,000 this year with the expectation of similar payments over the next four years. That would be like adding up a salary until a person retires and saying they just started a $5 million job, when they actually have to work 25 years to make that amount.

People say the numbers don't lie, but they lie all the time. You have to know how to decipher the code and figure out the truth. Most people are not interested in understanding accounting—except for accountants. They understand numbers and understand the games that people play. You should be aware of them, too. Don't let the exaggerations and overstatements people make about themselves affect how you feel about how you are doing in your own business. You may think everyone is so much more successful than you until you know what the numbers really do or don't represent.

34. Use the Rule of 72

Self-employed people have to do their own financial planning. You must set aside a large part of your money to grow, and to figure out how it will grow, you must understand the Rule of 72.

The Rule of 72 is a very important planning tool for calculating how long it will take money to double based on the interest rate you are paid. Dividing 72 by the interest rate gives you that approximate number. For example, an 8% return will double your money in 9 years (72 divided by 8), while a return of 2%, which is more normal for most people, will take 36 years (72 divided by 2). Focus on the returns generated by your capital because it really matters. This is useful for planning for retirement and other long-term strategic decisions.

35. Pay as Little Taxes as Possible

In the CPA business, they say that if you don't have a tax problem, then you have an income problem. That being said, the famous United States Appellate Court Judge Learned Hand said in 1947, "Anyone may arrange his affairs so that his taxes shall be as low as possible; he is not bound to choose that pattern which best pays the treasury. There is not even a patriotic duty to increase one's taxes. Over and over again, the courts have said that there is nothing sinister in so arranging affairs as to keep taxes as low as possible. Everyone does it, rich and poor alike, and all do right, for nobody owes any public duty to pay more than the law demands."

So step one: make more money; and step two: organize your affairs (under the watchful eye of an accountant and/or attorney) to pay the least amount of tax you can.

36. Which Tax System Are You Using?

We have two tax systems in the United States: one taxes earnings based on time, labor, and income-producing activities such as interest, dividends, rents, and royalties. The other system taxes growth of capital. Our labor system is generally called "ordinary income," and it can be taxed federally at up to 39%, plus whatever amount the state assesses. Profit on capital is called "capital gains tax", and it is taxed at 20%, plus some amount at the state level.

Warren Buffet frequently says it's not fair that he pays less tax than his secretary. But that's not exactly true. He does not pay less tax than his secretary, but he does pay at a lower tax *rate* because his money comes from capital and not from his labor or many ordinary activities. The question for you to consider: can you make it your goal to move to the capital gains system? Basically, can you create revenue streams in Box 3 and Box 4?

37. Make the Government Fund Your 401k

The maximum employee annual contribution (elective deferral) limit across all 401k plans for 2017 is $18,000. The maximum annual contribution for 2017 is $53,000, which includes elective deferrals, employer matching, and discretionary contributions, but excludes catch-up contributions for those over 50. For 2017, if a person is over 50 years of age, he or she can deduct up to $59,000 so an older taxpayer and spouse can receive up to $118,000 of tax-deferred money. There is no better tax shelter available to self-employed people than a 401k. I hope you are letting the government help fund your retirement. It's not easy to put the money away, but there is a pretty strong incentive to do so. Either save it, or give 40% or more of what you spend to the government, never to be seen again.

HARSH REALITIES

There is no gentle or PC way to say a few things that need to be said, but if you want to make real money, here are a few realities you must acknowledge.

38. Money Follows Expertise

I used to play professional blackjack on a team of card counters. That experience proved to me that if you get good enough, you can overcome all odds, including the Las Vegas house advantage. Money really does follow expertise. Companies pay extra for the best consultants (though I would argue that the best consultants and business talent are rarely located inside the nation's large consulting, accounting, and advisory firms. To understand why, go back and reread the very first insight, "Be a Great Street Fighter").

When you are really great at something, people seek you out. They need what you have. When you are *exceptionally* good—not just good, but *exceptional*—you are able to write your own ticket and charge what you feel you are worth for the problem you are solving.

To make sure you are always selling your highest and best service, my advice is to charge a lot for what you are good at and nothing for everything else. Don't fall into the trap of taking on jobs in areas that you are not an expert; just give that away. This forces you to stay focused and go deep in your most significant skillset. When you give advice away or a help with something that is outside your circle of expertise, you should keep expectations low. People get what they pay for. I am not suggesting that you not try your best; just don't charge for it. Charge your value for the things people know you for, and that you can consistently and confidently deliver.

Because money follows expertise, you will make up for any revenue you lose passing up jobs that aren't a match for your strongest skillset by just doing what you are really an expert in.

39. There's No Room for Schaumschlägers

At my seminars (and even inside my company), I always make sure that there are no Schaumschlägers anywhere. I say the word "Schaumschläger" during my presentations a few times before people in the audience finally ask what I am talking about. Then I proceed to explain:

I used to have a client who told a story about a guy who gets in a filled bathtub. He paddles and flails his arms at high speed and bubbles begin to build up in the water. Soon, the guy in the tub is overcome by bubbles—to the point where they are nearly covering his head. Exhausted, he gets out of the tub and dries himself off. When he turns around to look at the tub full of bubbles he so proudly created, what does he find? Nothing. The bubbles are all gone. That's a Schaumschläger: someone who is incredibly busy, but at the end of the day, has accomplished *nothing*.

After I tell the story, I usually ask if anybody in the audience has any experience with Schaumschlägers in their organization. The corporate people usually are quick to start giving up names of their time wasters and busybodies. One guy from a Fortune 500 recently told me that his company is the breeding ground for Schaumschlägers everywhere. On the other hand, there is no room for Schaumschlägers in the world in which entrepreneurs operate. Everyone in our world has to perform at top speed, and with great efficiency and productivity. Entrepreneurs eat only what we kill. We cannot afford to be slowed down by Schaumschlägers or worse— to become one.

You can avoid Schaumschlägers by asking yourself what you do to grow your business daily. Are you caught up in busy-ness or creating a business? My personal mission is to root out Schaumschlägers and make sure they are not part of businesses where I am involved. My goal is not to be busy; rather, my goal is to be productive. And in fact, my calendar is pretty light. I am not that busy—in part because the hours when I am working, I maintain a high yield so the rest of my day can be spent strategizing, planning, and thinking. I suggest you aim to do the same.

40. Rig the Rules

He who makes the rules, rigs the rules—not in an illegal way, but in a way that tilts the deal in his favor. So instead of sitting back and tolerating the rules others make, you need to start writing your own rules. Rich people write their rules—why shouldn't you? In fact, you might have heard of the golden rule in business: "he (or she) who has the gold makes the rules".

Consider the example of getting a voucher from an airline for a flight that has been cancelled. Can you use that voucher anytime? Can you transfer it to someone else? How long is it good for? Are there blackout dates? You better read the fine print, because the airlines create the rules on how and when that voucher can be used. And as you would expect, somehow, those rules tend to favor the airline.

That's just one example. Who decides on policies that govern your business? How easy is it to collect on an insurance policy or a home warranty plan? How do banks clear checks? What else is rigged in your world?

In Las Vegas, it's called the house advantage, and it's okay there because we expect it. But in life, we call it unfair. I'll say it again: he who writes the rules, rigs the rules. Who is writing the rules in *your* business and in your life? Who decides how payments are collected and when? Who decides what travel expense is or is not reasonable? Every interaction is governed by rules. Either you write those rules yourself, or you allow someone else to do it.

So start writing the rules. You need to rig them in your favor rather than being at the mercy of someone else's rules. For more on this, be on the lookout for my book *When it Comes to Money, Everything is Rigged.*

41. Don't Let Attorneys Kill Your Deals

An attorney's job is to protect their clients. But sometimes, they get too zealous—and they can create situations where the other party cannot say "yes". They believe they are helping, but sometimes they are *over*protective. When working on a deal with your attorney, you must regularly step back and ask if your position is reasonable from the perspective of the other party.

When attorneys give legal advice, you should take it. But sometimes they give business advice when they should not be giving business advice. Attorneys are not licensed to give out business advice and frequently they are not qualified to, but many do it anyway. As business people, *we* have to decide what is right for our businesses. *We* have to determine the right terms, timing, and circumstances that work for us and the other party; not our attorneys.

The goal of a negotiation and sale is to get the other party to say "yes", and if you over-complicate a proposal, this works against that goal by creating friction. To avoid that friction, be sure to understand the difference between legal and business advice. Keep things simple and keep friction to a minimum whenever possible.

42. Use a CPA, But Don't Expect Magic

CPAs have no special tricks. They aren't allowed to help you cheat. They all follow the same federal and state laws. The guidance all CPAs use comes from the same Internal Revenue Code, the same regulations, the same private letter rulings, and the same court cases. Your CPA cannot write new rules for you because you don't like the way the tax system works. In fact, there is not even legal privilege between you and your accountant, so if you are doing something bad, don't confide in the CPA because under oath, the CPA will have to spill the beans. Got it?

Hearing all of that, are you wondering if you should you use a CPA after all? I would ask you, do you know all of the tax codes, rules, regulations, and deductions possible for your business? Do you understand how your facts and circumstances compare to other businesses when making statements and claims? If not, leave do-it-yourself projects to home improvement. And don't leave home without a professional tax preparer.

43. Invest With Professional Investors

Professional investors bet on nearly sure things. We generally know exactly what we are doing and therefore, we make the money when we buy, not when we sell. Selling is just a matter of getting your cash out of the investment. A professional investor knows with near certainty what that amount will be. We know how we are going to get our money out of the investment before we go in. We understand the world in a different way than other investors. This is not about insider trading or anything improper. It's about the wisdom, experience, keen insight, and market intelligence that non-professionals don't have.

Retail investors rarely have enough information to be competitive. The system is rigged against you. Do not think that you can outsmart the system over the long term. You may succeed once or twice, but most of the time, retail investors might as well go to Las Vegas because they will have more fun losing their money. There is a reason that professional investors frequently make more money in 5 days than retail investors make in 5 years. I am a professional investor, so I can tell you with perfect certainty that this is true—and it's because we know more, we have been around the block more times, and because most of us leave gambling to boondoggles in Las Vegas!

Professional investors know how to invest with the market or against it. It does not matter if the market is up or down, we can see deals that glow in the dark and make decisions that—to a retail investor—may go against common sense or more likely, unnoticed.

There will come a time when you have money to invest. Educate yourself. Find a professional investor to get professional advice. Don't be stupid with your money; protect it. You know how hard you worked for it. Don't practice with your hard earned money; let a professional help you.

44. Don't Listen When They Tell You It's Too Hard

When someone tells you that something is too hard, they may be coming from one of a couple different directions:

> Whatever it is you are trying may be too hard for *them* to accomplish.

> They may tell you it is too hard for you and that you need their help.

The second reason is the one you have to watch out for because it can be manipulative and self-serving on their part. In some cases, maybe it is a hard task and you should hire someone else to do it, like doing your taxes or creating a killer website. You *could* do these tasks, but you might have to work really hard to accomplish them. You have to ask yourself whether it is worth the time and effort to gain a certain level of expertise or does it just make sense to hire someone to help?

There are some things people say are too hard, but may not be—for instance, self- publishing. Sure there are some things you may need some help with, but to open an account and put your book up online with a print on demand publisher is really not as difficult as you might think.

The bottom line is that you need to be the one to determine whether something is too hard or not to accomplish and shut out the naysayers. They either know your potential and support you, or it's possible they have an ulterior motive to keep you from being your best.

45. Don't Put Your Problems Out of Sight or Mind

Don't believe anything you hear, and only half of what you see. Financial problems are invisible, and as a society, we go out of our way to hide these problems. The people you think have a lot of money may have less than you think. Other people you believe are your friends may abandon you if they find out you have financial problems. If you have these problems, do not let them fester. Get help. Share the problem. Ask for assistance in drawing up a plan to resolve the problem. If you lose a few "friends" along the way because they do not want to be with someone who struggles financially, then they were not your friends to begin with. Find new and better friends.

You may not know how to address whatever issue you have—and the facts and circumstances of your particular situation will dictate the correct course of action, but there is a solution to every problem. Put these issues behind you by taking bold and smart actions now. Find help. Get support. Get over the hump. Your new, unshackled self will thank you.

46. Understand the Financial Reports

Becoming financially literate may not be the most fun part of running your business, but I can assure you, if you don't understand your financial reports, you won't be in business for very long.

When I was chairman of the board, many members of my Los Angeles Boys & Girls Club board of directors did not know how to read the financial statements that were provided to them each month. So each meeting, I spent some time reviewing the reports with the group, and I also always shared insights that only a trained eye would notice. There were a few people who were not happy with the "lessons" I shared. They just were not interested in learning about or understanding financial materials. My advice to those people was to leave the board because as fiduciaries, we have a responsibility they could not fulfill without financial insights.

You have a similar duty to yourself and your family. You must understand your financial information—like it or not. Period.

There is a lot of information in the financial reports—and in the reports from your own QuickBooks or from your own tax returns—and these documents are hard to read and understand. Get some help. Learn this material.

But keep in mind that understanding financial basics, such as the information in the financial reports, is just the beginning and not the same as understanding the money. Money is a much more advanced topic, while financial reports are just a detailed review of the historical performance of the business. But you have to start your education somewhere. Remember, you can't control what you don't understand, right?

47. Work With People Who Have the Money to Pay

Doing business with individuals and companies who have the money to pay for your services may seem obvious, but I have found that self-employed people spend a lot of time talking to a potential client only to find out that they have no money. They are disappointed to find out the huge opportunity is non-paying.

The issue is that a lot of service providers don't often like to talk about money. They feel it is premature to discuss the money matters upfront, so they are disappointed on the backend. Isn't your time worth more than that? There are some situations in which you can work with a client to be paid in other ways and make deals, such as trading services, or even a guarantee of being booked later for bigger and more extended pay.

You should talk about money early. You can say things such as, "Are you aware of my fee?" Have the conversation and own it. Spend your time and effort on those who can afford you.

You have to get out of the mindset of desperation of taking just anything - know your value and demand payment for it!

And for the record, the most successful business owners have mastered this conversation. They are not embarrassed by their fee, nor are they reluctant to discuss it. You don't think the person you are talking to about engaging you is working free, do you?

48. Take the Bull by the Horns: Strategic Planning

Each day, we face stressful business situations. And each time, these obstacles either bully and taunt us or propel us forward in ways that we can't imagine. Sadly, many of us routinely find ourselves in situations where we are caught off guard and have to react impulsively. The bull attacks and we get gored. Frequently, it happens over and over again because we react spontaneously to these situations instead of learning from past mistakes and making big changes.

Any time you fail to take charge, you go back into the arena to fight the same bull. However, if you take the bull by the horns and proactively implement an appropriate strategy, you'll be amazed by how quickly you can beat the bull and launch that success into bigger and better ones.

Sometimes we learn our business lessons from simple life experiences. My favorite example of a personal situation where I took the bull by the horns and developed a strategy to solve a specific problem happened in my pre-marital days. One date in particular taught me a business lesson about proactivity that I'll never forget.

My twenty-something dating ritual usually consisted of picking my date up, taking her to dinner, and driving her home. I thought it would be a good way to get to know someone, but the results were never that great. Then one fateful evening, I went on a date with a woman, and the outcome forced me to re-examine my ritual and what I wanted to accomplish.

Toward the end of the meal, my date mentioned to our waiter that it was her birthday. The servers responded with usual birthday hoopla - complete with whooping, hollering, and clapping. Then the waiter then leaned forward and asked me, "What's the birthday girl's name?"

There the bull was… snorting at me with its flared nostrils, ready to gore me, waiting for the million-dollar answer. My palms started to sweat and my eyes dropped to my lap as I realized that I couldn't remember her name. I drew a complete blank. Confused, panicked, and embarrassed, I reacted the way any person in that situation would: I pretended to not hear the waiter. Each time the waiter asked me for her name, I felt the bull's horns getting closer and closer to me as I cupped my ear and asked him to repeat the question. Finally, in a huff, my date blurted out her name to the waiter. We sang, we ate the birthday dessert, and we had a very quiet and long ride home.

Shaken up by this experience, I regrouped and developed a "dating strategy." The next time I went out, I decided to make reservations at a nice restaurant that was about an hour away. That way, my date and I would have a chance to get to know each other on the drive there. If we hit it off, then we would go have dinner. If not, we would just grab a drink, and I'd take her home. On my next date, I put a permanent leash on my bull. I picked my date up and we proceeded to drive to the restaurant. We hit it off immediately and had a great time talking in the car. The dinner went just as well. Because I didn't let the bull take me, that woman—Sandy - and I have been married for 27 years now.

The point is this: I had a bad experience, and I had to take that bull by the horns to ensure success. People don't always do that in business, although they should. They don't actually sit down after the bull charges them to debrief and figure out what they did wrong. If you have a myopic view of the bull, chances are, you're not going to know which direction it's charging or whether it's charging at you at all. If you don't step back, take a deep breath, and get some clarity on things, you won't be able to find out what went wrong, much less get better results the next time around. The bull will gore you over and over again until a) the bull renders you insolvent or b) you develop a proactive strategy to defeat it.

SALES WAGS THE DOG – NOT THE OTHER WAY AROUND

Those of us who are sales-oriented tend to believe that sales is the most important skill a business person can possess, and I have to admit, I am one of those people. Just look around. Who are the most successful people among us? It is not necessarily the most talented people. Rather, it is the people who are the best at telling prospects how they can add value to their situation. Master your selling skills, and watch the demand for your other skills soar.

49. All Business People Should Be CSPs

My friend Michelle Villalobos calls speaking "the new marketing" which says to me that all successful business owners must be "communicators who solve problems". The bigger the problem you can solve, the more money the client will pay you. Speeches and other forms of marketing don't solve problems the way advisory or consulting services do, but they can open the minds of the audience members to be ready to accept changes that will make an organization better. The two concepts of speaking and consulting therefore go hand in hand. Learn how to sell both and to bring value by delivering both to your clients. This is a huge money-making formula.

50. Nobody Wants What You are Selling

It is very unlikely that anybody wants the "thing" you are selling. People don't want things. They want feelings, outcomes, and accomplishments. Marketers call those "benefits". Things have "features", which is not what people buy. They may eventually pay for those features because they believe it will help them achieve the outcomes they want, but without selling the "other side of the river", it is hard to get people to buy the stepping stones.

It is my experience that no one *wants* to buy the stepping stones to get to the other side of the river, but they will pay for them if they *really* want to get to the other side of the river. No one wants to buy a website, but they will pay for it if they want the outcomes that a great website can deliver. No one wants to pay for the services of an accountant or attorney, but they agree to it so that they can receive the outcome those professionals deliver.

The way that I know if I am selling benefits instead of features is by connecting the concepts with the phrase "So That". It is very simple and it works like this: instead of saying, "buy this pen", try "buy this pen so that you can sign giant checks with flair and confidence." Get the point? You will notice that from time to time throughout this book, I have used the phrase "so that" to drive a few of my points home. Try it. It works like a charm!

51. Sell Their Dream Back to Them

Sell your vision of what is possible if "we" (you and your prospective client) work together. There is a great distinction that many people miss. Remember you are selling "the other side of the river". Keep the client focused on what they want and where they are going, and then you will start seeing how you are going to be with them at the finish line.

Talk about what is possible. Talk about what you can do together once you start working together. You want to sell their vision back to them—you are not creating an alternate reality. Sometimes it works out, sometimes it doesn't, but as long as you try your best, and as long as accomplishing what you promised is inside of you expertise, then you are on the right track.

You have to find out what the client wants, and sell that. If it is teamwork, then you are selling teamwork. Find out what their vision and desire is and lock onto that.

This strategy tends to work best with high-level people who are responsible for initiatives such as some aspect of vision for the organization. Trying to understand the vision and locking onto it will probably not work well if you're dealing with administrative and middle management level people.

Finally, keep this in mind: the possibilities—and therefore your value—are never greater than before you launch. Once live, the reality—even if great—is never as good as the dream. The same is true for that car you wanted so badly. Once you get whatever it was you dreamed of, it may not be as special as you imagined. The dream phase is your time to make a giant sale. The goal is not to sell what you can do, rather how you can help your client to achieve *their* goal.

52. Make Your First Sale a Giant Sale

Whenever you start a brand new company, you have an opportunity that you will never have again, and that is to make your first sale a giant sale. People look at me cross-eyed, like I'm from outer space when I suggest this. They frequently say, "Joel, duh, of course we want to make our first sale a giant sale, but I'm lucky to make *any* sale."

Making any sale isn't the point in a brand new business, especially one that is entrepreneurially-driven and that has lots of startup cachet. If you come up with a great idea and you frame the great idea in a way that other people want it, especially a large company, then your likelihood for making a giant first sale is very real.

Sell the vision before you launch, because once you launch, you will either achieve the vision, or not. But even if you do, the vision is always more exciting than the reality.

When I first started my new media publishing company known by the brand name Financial Fax in 1992, I created a story that our personal faxing service could create personalized newspapers for investors who read stock tables. That was enough to get the Los Angeles Times to jump over themselves and be the first one in the industry, and they wrote a very sizable check to become my backer. Then I took that concept to Wall Street, and I got Prudential Securities to purchase the exclusive rights to send out our personal financial newspaper to their clients, because no one had ever seen anything like it. The response by Prudential was "wow, we need this". They didn't want a competitor to have it; they wanted it for themselves because there was so much interest, cachet, and prestige potentially associated with this product.

Some years later, I got involved with a startup construction company, and they had created the concept of replacing plastic spacers for guys who laid tile. It was about the most mundane concept you could come up with. Their concept was to replace those plastic spacers with spacers made out of the same thinset material that the grout was set between already. Therefore, you didn't have to remove the little spacers after applying the grout. We went to a trade show and spoke to the five largest companies in the industry. We told them the idea, and we got interest from the biggest one in the industry.

When we saw that company shortly after the show, the vice president we sat with uttered words that I could only dream of—and had never heard anyone say before. From his words, I knew that we could write our own ticket to close the transaction. He told me that some years before, somebody brought him a cool idea. He didn't jump on it and it cost him market share, and then he said the magic words, and I quote, "and I'll never let that happen again". Once he said that, I knew there was no reasonable limit to the number we could ask for, and he wrote a check that was so big it started our little factory with 10 people who were busy producing thinset spacers for almost eight months nonstop. Plus, it covered all the past due bills and it got the company rolling.

Fast forward to 2015, when I started InvestorValet. And when I shared the vision with a large brokerage firm on the east coast, they said the magic words, "Wow, we need that network you've built". And once they said that, I knew that we could pretty much work out the monetary arrangements to create a new relationship with this company, which is exactly what has happened.

If you have a vision, use words like, "imagine if" or "listen up". If you can describe your concept in a way that makes a larger company want to keep it all for themselves, they will pay you handsomely for it. Knowing how to precisely put the package together—that's a special skill. You have to create the story and the vision for what your product could be and how you're going to actualize your product or service. If you can make the sale, you can get help constructing the transaction either from an attorney or from some other adviser.

But I want you to think carefully about the idea of making a giant first sale. One of the things that I've done in my career over and over again when I started really cool entrepreneurial companies is "make the first sale a giant sale". And again, it may sound obvious, but common sense is not common practice and in my experience, it's pretty rare for someone to launch a company using this approach.

When you are brokering a deal with a company to provide services, you want to sell them the biggest package possible because you may not get another opportunity in the future. Sell them on the idea and concept that they need you for multiple talks rather than one. They need you for team coaching of all the departments, not one. You need to coach all the executives, not just one.

53. Sell Nouns

People buy nouns. Nouns are what we all learned about in the third grade, but they are so simple nothing can compare. A noun is something people can see in their mind's eye. Most people hate consulting, but they love well-defined programs with names. I don't sell open-ended consulting by the hour with an imaginary goal. I sell specific deliverables whenever possible for a fixed fee. For example, I sell a "Finish Line" or an "Organizational Bullseye™". It is a productized package that includes a clear and specific outcome. It is something they can see in their mind; something tangible. People say, "I want one of those" or "that's exactly what we need". They want a specific outcome—a dot on the wall—a noun. A process is not a noun and not something people usually want. Sell an outcome. If you are selling a service package, give it a name people can relate to. Give all of your products great names. Help your prospects imagine themselves attaining the outcome.

54. Sell the Other Side of the River

Don't sell the stepping stones to get to other side of the river; sell the other side of the river. Prospects want the glory and excitement that waits for them there. They will buy the stones if they really want to get to the other side, but your focus should be the other side. That is your selling point. Describe the other side of the river in great detail, get the prospect to buy into the ideas—or better yet, use their own ideas and parrot them back to them.

How does the client see themselves? How do they see a particular process going? Get them to envision the outcome as an achievement, which would be their "other side of the river". Get them excited about it.

Think about it this way. If you walk into a luxury car dealership, they do not start off with financing terms or cost. They want you to test drive the car and become excited about it. They want you to see yourself as the owner of that new high end car. Once they have sold that, the rest comes much easier. And remember, nobody wants the stepping stones, but they will tolerate them if they believe it will take them to the other side of the river.

No one wants your products or services. They want the outcome on the other side of the river. And they will buy what you sell to help them get there.

55. Make People Beg to Be Your Customer

Get people to beg to be your customer. Stop selling. Start telling. Make your buyers qualify to work with you. You must give people parameters. To join my programs, I give prospects three criteria that they need to meet in order to qualify to attend my conference. It is amazing; once they hear the parameters, people try to sell me on all the ways they meet the necessary criteria. They want in, and they sell me on the idea that they are a good candidate. I did not establish the criteria for this purpose, but it has certainly gone a long way in creating lots of buyers.

Try to position yourself the opposite way of being a commodity. You want them to beg you to be a part of you event. Create criteria for you to provide your talk to their audience. This is how you create buyers.

56. Be a Snake Charmer: Pluck Perfect Prospects

This works best if you're giving a talk or presentation of some sort, but you can even work it into personal conversations. Your goal is to find prospects who you know will be interested in what you have to sell. One technique I use during big talks is the following:

"For those interested in learning more on this subject, my office has produced a white paper on the material. After my talk, bring me your business card and write 'WP' for white paper on it. When I return, I will have my office send you the paper."

By bringing me a card, the true prospects have just revealed themselves to me. These are the people I know are potential clients, even though they only represent a portion of the room.

Once we get the cards, we scan the cards and import them into our funnel of people who are in sync and interested in the material I presented. The goal is not to get every card, but rather to get a slice of the attendees—those who are most interested in the specific product or services offering that you provide.

If you're just talking with someone one-on-one, and you have a white paper or article that pertains to the topic they seem interested in, you can do the same.

57. Sell to Pain

Fear, uncertainty, and doubt—(FUD): people are consumed by it. I heard somewhere that Americans take 10 times more pain pills than vitamins. Whether that's actually true or not, we can still leverage and take a lesson from that; we can sell to the client's pain. They don't need help for the areas that are going great. They need help to correct deficiencies and problems that could fester into full-blown disasters. I don't sell happy times and Kumbaya; I get clients to see what will happen if we don't engage. The ones who imagine a world without my solution are the ones who say "yes". It's important to know that I don't stomp my feet or raise my voice. I am very calm. I stay rational—remember, I am a CPA by training. In a very ironic way, the calmness is sometimes what's most disturbing to the client. After all, their problem is not my problem; my life is going great. I'm not the one who is going to lose his job, or company, or family.

When you identify the pain point, you have to continue poking at it by repeatedly asking questions about the problem to solidify your understanding of it. After a while, the prospect will scream and beg for your help to make the problem go away.

I was in the hospital some years ago, and when the doctor came, he started poking around on my belly until he hit a spot that made me scream. He promptly went back and poked the same spot again, which caused another outburst from me. Then he jokingly told me not to ever scream in front of a doctor because it makes the doctor want to poke in the same place again. Be like a doctor. Poke around. Keep poking until the screams get loud and then offer the perfect solution to take away the pain.

Talking about issues that are painful—including issues that bring up fear, uncertainty, or doubt—make prospects take a second look, because no one wants to make a mistake on purpose.

58. Disqualify Before You Qualify

People so often ask what makes me a good seller and how it is that I have such a good "batting average" when it comes to selling. The answer is rather simple. I am rational and provide reasonable, thoughtful answers to the questions people ask me. I don't use gimmicks or goofy strategies that people can spot from a mile away.

In short, I don't do what I don't like people doing to me. But my batting average is so high also because my approach is fully based on a substantive technique that I call "Disqualify Before You Qualify". Every sales course, book, and training teaches how to qualify a prospect—and this is a critical step in any successful sales encounter. If the prospect isn't qualified to do business with you, then they won't buy. But there is a whole step before the qualification step, and if you do that first step right, you will save so much time and so much energy that your personal batting average will skyrocket.

That first step requires that you know who you want your customer to be—and "someone with money" is not the right answer. First, define the perfect customer. Then, come up with questions to find him or her (some of these questions should also help you determine whether the person you are speaking with is worth moving forward with or not). Remember, the more specific you are, the more likely you are to be successful.

ALWAYS ADD VALUE

If you want to make your job as a salesperson as easy as sales can be (which does not mean it will be easy), show your clients and customers exactly how you will add value to their situation. Draw a line between your services and the prospect's ability to improve his or her organization, and you will demonstrate that you are a valuable asset for the team. When you fail to do that, you have only demonstrated that your participation doesn't matter that much.

59. Your Value Is All About Perception

"Beauty is in the eye of beholder." "One man's trash is another man's treasure" (or in a business context, "one man's trash is another man's cash"). These clichés illustrate that perception determines the true value of something. *You* may have sense of your own value, but your job is to convince *others* of it. You have to temper your expectations with what others perceive your value to be.

You may have worked 50 years in marketing, but does that make you a great trainer on the subject of advertising? Unless you can demonstrate how your experience has value and how your training has value, there will be a conflict between what you perceive your value to be, and what others perceive it to be. And when there is a mismatch, you lose gigs.

If you are looking for bigger money, dedicate yourself to delivering greater value and creating that perception of value so you can communicate it to those you are negotiating with.

60. Keep Adding Value to the Deal

The number of dollars you make is directly proportionate to the value you bring. If you solve a small problem, you get a small fee, and if it is a larger one, you make more. When you go to the movies, you pay your ten dollars, sit for two hours, and are entertained for a short while. As a speaker, let's say you get $10,000 for a thousand-member audience. Your value to the buyer is therefore about $10 a person. If, however, you make the same rate but only have 500 people in the audience, then the perceived value by the buyer goes up to $20 a person—making you a higher value on a per-attendee basis to the client. Of course, the same is true in the other direction: if you are making $5K and are speaking to a 1,000 person audience, then your value is a bargain matinee price of $5 per person.

Think about how you can add more value to bring a higher fee. What problem can you solve or address that is worth more to the client? This is a good question for speakers but it's a *critical* one for consultants and authors because it opens the door to really big ticket advisory services. Find the problem and bring value by solving it. That's the big money formula.

61. Focus on Needs

Stop focusing on the products you sell and start focusing on the strategic needs of your clients. Only when you focus on their problems and their needs will the money stop trickling and start pouring in.

Unless you understand the client's problems, how can you evaluate and value your contribution to the solution? Once you are able to determine the value of your solution, you will be in a strong position to make a large sale by connecting the dots of your solution to an economic gain for the client. Once you do this, your fee—which should be just a fraction of the economic value of the solution to the client—will be easy for them to swallow. Give it a try. You'll be surprised by the results.

62. Make Them Choose the Average

When I ask investors to place money in my fund, they ask how much it costs to buy in to join the fund. I generally tell them the minimum is

$50,000, but on average, investors put in between $100,000 and $300,000. No one wants to be the low end of the range. People feel comfortable and want to be in the middle, so they will typically invest around $150,000.

When people are talking to you about your rates or cost of your services, you can tell them the same thing (always be truthful based on your situation): "the least expensive package is $8,000, but on average, people in our programs are in the $12,000 to $15,000 dollar range." This is just my observation about life, but people will often gravitate to the middle. It seems rare for people to want you at the bottom of your range because they don't want to appear cheap, or they may be concerned about not getting your best effort. And most will not want to go overboard and purchase at the top of your range. It's funny how people are, but they are pretty predictable.

63. Leave Your Village

The Bible astutely points out that "no man is a prophet in his own village". In a business context, that means that you should book gigs out of town to get bigger paydays. It's all about perception and the creation of value. People get excited when someone comes in from out of town. If you want to maximize your fees, you must look past your local market. You seem to be something special and can create a mystique when you come from another location. The perception is that people who fly in to provide services are more valuable than those that live in your community. And your billing rate will reflect it. And since perception is reality, cater to the perception.

64. Be Exact

In selling consulting or other services, tell people *exactly* what will happen or what they will get. Suppose someone asks you what they are going to get if they hire you as a consultant. You don't want to say, "well, you are going to pay me; then I'm going to do some work, and then we'll see what happens."

That is infuriating to clients, but many service providers convey a similar message. You want to be clear and specific about what you are offering and about the outcome, if that's possible.

Instead, you could say, "I have seen the situation your company is in a hundred times, and I know *exactly* what to do to solve the problem. I am going to help you by doing the following... and that is going to cost you this much". When you use the word "exactly", it changes the dynamic. It instills trust and confidence in what you are going to provide. It further positions you as a significant authority on the topic or problem, which is what people with problems want. Clients want problems to go away and your job is to make prospects feel like you are the exact right person to make that happen.

65. Don't Think - KNOW

To piggyback on the last insight, never use the words "I think". It usually means you have no idea and that you are making it up as you go along. It is the opposite of the word "exactly". You want to instill confidence. Words matter. When you say, "I know" with authority, it means you don't really have to think about the answer, you already know it. When you are confident, your client will be confident and trust in you more.

The more specific you are, the more confidence your client will have in you. How do you like it when someone waffles when trying to figure out the solution to a problem? That's right—you don't.

66. Help Clients CYA

Every employee is concerned about covering his or her behind, so if you can help someone CYA (Cover Your A...), you will be well received. Early technology managers bought IBM computers, not because they were the best, but because they could later go to the boss if there were problems and use the IBM defense. In other words, "we bought IBM. What more could we have done?"

Similarly, there are many professional associations that offer certification to those that meet a high standard and criteria. These are the crème de la crème. They have the experience, the feedback, and are respected in the community.

Suppose your potential client is choosing between you and several other vendors. If one of you has a certification or special designation or extra license, can you guess whom they are more likely to choose? They don't want to fail, so they are going to choose the person that is the better bet—if only to cover their own butt.

The moral: if certifications and designations are available in your industry, getting one or more of them will probably pay off handsomely.

PROSPECTING PERFECT PROSPECTS

67. Look for Left-Handed Plumbers

The more that you can describe your business with specificity, the better off your business will be. Specifics help people know what your skills are and what you have to offer. If they match what people are looking for, or it hits a pain point for them, they will more often engage with you, versus if your offerings are vague. Vague descriptions produce vague results. And that hurts your wallet. But don't worry about pigeonholing yourself; people are very good at extrapolating and digging deeper when they are truly interested.

Suppose an accountant goes to a cocktail party and someone asks her what she does.

"I am an accountant," the woman replies.

"Oh really, what kind of accountant are you? Do you specialize in any area?"

"As a matter of fact I do. I work mostly with left-handed plumbers. Do you know any left handed plumbers?"

The person thinks a bit and says, "Well, I don't know any left-handed plumbers, but I might know some right-handed plumbers. Do you work with any of those?"

"Well sure, I mean plumbers are plumbers, and their accounting issues are very similar."

Another person overhears the conversation, and says, "I don't know any plumbers but I know some fencing contractors, do you work with any of those?"

She replies, "Sure, because I find that contractors all have similar financial situations. Plumbers fall into contracting just like fencing contractors do."

People have an easier time generalizing from the narrow to the broad than the other way around. Let the people you are talking about figure out how to expand your service to their need.

If I were to ask you to list all of the restaurants in your neighborhood, this may be a difficult task. If I asked you to list all the Chinese restaurants in your neighborhood, this is a much easier mental task. People have an easier time conceptualizing specific things and going outward, than they do going from generalized to specific.

You may be able to offer different services, but you should only advertise your top three areas of expertise. Then when someone is looking for the skills you have, they may see what you offer, and ask you whether you have other skills as well.

Describe what you do for a specific audience or type of organization and let the prospect imagine how you can similarly deliver a message to a different or broader one. Because the problems of one audience may be similar to another, once you get into a company and they know you, they will share you between departments and give you more business.

68. Choose Clients That Are Easy to Find

If you are working too hard to find clients, you are probably targeting the wrong group of people, and your niche is too small. Good clients or prospects have a few key attributes in common. First, as I have already said, they have the money to buy your products and/or services. Secondly, they should be abundant—at least abundant enough for you to build a business that is satisfactory for your goals or your needs. And finally, they should be easy to find.

Finding prospects usually involves marketing dollars, but if your marketing budget is very small, you should make them easy to find using a low-cost marketing system, such as a referral network. If you are unable to find quality prospects and clients given the budget and resources available to you, then you need to rethink your business, your target audience, your budgets, or all of the above.

69. Find Problems That Are a Perfect Fit

Just because someone is desperate for help, it does not mean you are the right person to solve the problem; however, you should be on the lookout for those problems for which you *are* the perfect person to provide the solution. I was consulting for a company that was desperate and on its knees—and running out of money fast. They needed immediate solutions, and I knew I could help them.

When I took the assignment, I didn't know the solution to the problem, but I knew exactly *how* to go about *finding* the solution. I had been down the path many times before.

The company cleaned toxic water using a revolutionary, new approach. I wrote the problem on a 3x5 card and asked everyone I saw what they thought. My 3x5 card asked the question, "what company has toxic water problems that without which, could generate billions of dollars?" The best suggestion came from a friend who suggested cleaning the water left behind after recycling plastic water bottles, but I got dozens of ideas. All of them were fantastic solutions that I eventually compiled and shared with the company.

There are many service providers that go around and say, "I can do that" to any problem. The reality is that no one can solve all problems. Figure out what you can and can't solve, and you will excel in your field. If you take the "I can do that" approach to everything, you will dilute your credibility and potentially destroy the focus of your business.

When you can demonstrate that you are the solution to a company's problem, you can be very successful. Ask yourself what problem can you solve, and why you are the best person to solve it.

70. Find What You Seek

How often do you see a yellow car? Probably not often, unless you *are* looking. But when you are looking, you see them everywhere. Each of us has to define what our "yellow car" is. For me, it is primarily investors. For you, it might be the people who need speakers, meeting planners, or business executives. These people may not be obvious, but they gather in specific places; we just have to get into the habit of looking for them and finding ways to determine who they are and where they go. I find my yellow cars by asking simple questions or by providing leading answers to questions a person might ask me.

At the base of our brains is the Reticular Activating System (RAS). It is responsible for our sleep cycles, but it has an even more important function while we are awake. At all times, your brain receives millions of pieces of information through your senses. We cannot focus on everything at once, so the information is passed through the RAS. The RAS is like a mail sorter—it judges the information as something important or not important.

Try this little experiment. You receive information about your toes all the time. Without moving your feet, concentrate on what your toes feel like right now. If you sense nothing, wiggle your toes. Now you are aware of what your toes feel like. But even when you are not paying attention to your toes, the information is still being sent to your brain; it's just eventually sorted out as not important.

You can use this to your advantage, because you constantly program your RAS to give you the information you seek - sometimes on purpose, sometimes not. If you are driving in hazardous conditions, your RAS is sending you as much visual information that it can. You become focused on the road in order to respond.

This is the trick of the yellow car. When you suddenly start seeing them more, it is not as though yellow cars are surging in popularity; it is your RAS sending and flagging that information for you. They have always been there; you just notice them more often now.

Once you start looking for yellow cars, you will see one (or more) every day. Start looking for business opportunities—they are everywhere. When you activate your RAS in your business, you become acutely aware of new opportunities. Use this to your advantage. Program your RAS to be aware of things you want to be aware of.

71. Wait Until You Are Asked

When creating new relationships, you have to assume no one cares about what you have to say, at least until they ask. If you begin talking before people ask, you may be sorely disappointed in the results. The less you say in the beginning, the more they will want to know. If you begin by blabbering about yourself before anyone shows interest, you may turn them off, and therefore kill an opportunity to connect. In fact, the only way to know someone is interested in what you have to say is by their *questions*. No questions, no interest. It's that simple. When introducing yourself, make statement that creates curiosity. Statements of fact are boring and do not create the give and take of a healthy conversation. Craft statements that make a person ask, "how do you do that"?

For example, when someone asks me what I do, I will usually say, "I run a hedge fund that buys real estate across the country and we share the profits with our investors." There is usually one of three common responses to that. First, someone might say, "Interesting, do you know what the weather will be in Milwaukee next week?" I never pursue people who are not interested. Or, they might ask if they can sell me some real estate. Once I know the person is a vendor, I can have an appropriate conversation. Or finally, they might ask, "How can I get in on a deal like that"? Those people are prospects—and they identify themselves every time. When it happens to you, just listen to their questions, and remember, play it cool.

NEGOTIATE YOUR WAY TO WHATEVER YOU WANT

Nobody ever offers us exactly what we are worth in exactly the way we want it. We have to take what comes at us and reshape it in a way that works for us. That process is negotiation. It is not complicated and it doesn't have to be formal. But if you don't ask, and if you don't stick up for yourself, who will? Get in the habit of getting crystal clear about what you want, what you need and how important these elements are to you. Then be prepared to discuss ways to get what matters to you while giving what matters to the other party. As they say, if you don't know where you are going, anywhere will do. Always know where you want to go in a negotiation.

Libraries have been written on this topic but here are a few pointers from my experience.

72. Use the Magic Word

As kids, the magic word was "please", but as business people, the magic word is "no". Always be able to say no. Otherwise, you are unable to negotiate. When we are just starting out and you have little or no money, we tend to take whatever we can get—which is why this material is for people that already have a lot of momentum. The more you say no, the more likely you are to see your success escalate.

73. Sacrifice Short-Term Gains for Long-Term Gains

It's important for all of us to open our minds, believe we're worthy of charging for our value, and capitalize on opportunities as they come. When the opportunity to really make some money appears, most people do not optimize it because they don't know how to do it.

For example, you might open your mind to the possibility of making more money, but then you end up just getting more money for one job or engagement. Although you feel good because you raised your fee, your hourly yield (or the amount you make divided by the amount of time it actually takes to generate the money) might still only be mediocre. However, if you understood more about how to construct recurring and passive income streams, then you might be able to do better. I always look for these opportunities whenever possible, and that's the reason why—rather than taking an opportunity where I'm paid a fee just for service with a relatively low yield—I'll usually opt for something that has a larger opportunity in the long run, such as participation via percentage of success or company stock. This might mean you make less money in the short run to make more in the long run. Think about plaintiff attorneys taking a percentage of the recovery. If those guys are good, and if they pick good cases, they can make a lot of dough. This strategy is not for everyone, but it can work really well for many people.

74. Look for Prospects on Their Knees

When people say that they don't have any money, what they may be saying is that they don't have any money for *you*. They may have money for other things, but you are not a priority to that prospect. Sorry—sometimes the truth hurts.

Prospects always have the money. But having money in the bank and giving it to you are not related. There are a lot of broke people who make bail. What more do I need to say?

The strategy is to find the prospects who are already on their knees that you can help. And sometimes that means looking a little deeper than the surface: the company might be fine, but a department, manager, or a product line might be doing badly. Those people are the ones who will see your value and will pay you handsomely for helping to make the problem go away. FYI, don't *put* them on their knees so you make them need you, as that is illegal (I am pretty sure that solving a problem that you create is racketeering, so don't do that). I am not suggesting that you strong arm anyone, either. Find prospects who are hurting and work to help them benefit from your assistance. Find out what people need and provide them the assistance you can offer to meet that need.

Look for clients that need you the most. The problem is that many self-employed people are so hungry that when any client offers them money for a project, too many people will take it, rather than holding out for their "target" audience. This might provide a short-term cash flow solution, but it does little to really build your brand and reputation. And because it is not your target audience, it might be harder work. Also remember: targets are not stationary, so the right clients are subjective and can change over time.

BUSINESS PHILOSOPHIES AND OBSERVATIONS

I have a few philosophies that have guided me through my career and perhaps they will help to shape some of your positions, too. For example, I have noticed that many professional service providers struggle financially, but they fight to keep up a high-flying image for peers and prospects. Just look at the cars accountants, attorneys, and real estate brokers drive. Whether they can afford the car or not, there is a belief that a powerful look will make the difference. And maybe that is true—or maybe it's not. Consider your beliefs and philosophies while you look at some of mine.

75. Don't Be Afraid to Be Contrarian

When everybody is going to the right, I usually go to the left, and I highly suggest that you look at the world differently from other people. That is what thought leaders do. They often see opportunities others miss or dig deeper than the rest. My selling philosophies tend to be different than most, but that does not mean what others say does not work. They tend to open the door for a good debate, however.

While I don't go out of my way to make people mad, I subscribe to a philosophy to deal with our politically correct world: *If you don't offend someone, then you affect no one.* I share my opinion and I try to be pretty clear about it and I don't worry about someone not liking it because inevitably, someone won't agree. My comments are nearly always business-oriented and I work hard to never tease or pick on people for things out of their control, nor for personal issues. My opinions are not about personal aspects of people's lives—I'm about money and business. But there is still a lot of room for thought-provoking commentary and healthy disagreement.

Even if the crowd is going one way, that does not mean you have to go in that direction if you see it a different way. Keep in mind, I am not contrarian for the sake of being contrarian; I am contrarian when being so works, like when I see the potential in a deal that goes against typical practice. Consider Austin, Texas. There is a saying out there - "Keep Austin Weird". Some people may act weird or strange there, but they are usually very average, normal people. It seems to me, they are doing it for the sake of being weird—or so they can say they are weird. That sounds contrarian for the sake of being so, which is not my style. To me, weird is Venice Beach, California. That is a really weird place and the people are not making it up. They are just being themselves.

76. Don't Overthink Your Business Plan

There are two different kinds of business plans that most organizations deal with: an internal plan and an external one. An internal plan is what is created between the partners in the company. An external plan is one that is shown to others, such as outside investors.

Not every organization needs an external plan, as you usually only use these when you're trying to get funding from investors or loans from lenders. It shows what you do and how you intend to make money and how you will pay them back. These are known as "investment grade plans", and can be quite formal, lengthy, and detailed.

Internal plans, on the other hand, are essential. But don't worry; they don't have to be complicated—in fact, it can begin with an outline that you just write out on a napkin.

The three questions you need to answer in order to build a great internal business plan are:

> What is the problem?
> What is my solution?

> Why am I the best person to provide this solution?

Then there are a few follow up questions such as, "how will I monetize this opportunity?" If you do not know how to monetize your business, you may need to seek external help through books, classes, coaches, or consultants.

Remember that business is simple, so describe yours in simple terms. The basis of a business can be about getting someone to pay you money to make a problem go away. When you figure out what problems you help make go away, and how to do it, you have the foundation of not only your business plan, but of your business as a whole. Then start focusing on how you will let people know you are available to make their problems go away.

77. Assess Your Ideas

The hallmark of a great idea is *one that gets bigger with every person who touches it.* You'll know when you create a great idea because people that encounter it will ask, "Can we do this with it?" The idea will grow with each person who is in contact with it. If the idea is a dud, it will get smaller because people will not be interested in it. One way to determine whether an idea is good or not is to study other people's feedback and actions when you tell them about it. If they are excited by it, want to talk about it, or maybe even want to invest in it, then these are indicators you have a winner. Spend your time on great ideas, and ditch those that don't excite anyone but you.

78. Focus, Focus, Focus

We love experts. We pay big bucks to watch professional sports, courts of law count on expert testimony, and companies pay premium fees for the best talent. The opportunities are out there for you, too—get rich in your niche! Generalists rarely make big money—no one is an expert and knows everything about everything. Focus, Focus, Focus. Stay on target on with whatever you are great at. Get really good at your special area and the money will begin to flow. Why? People don't want you to practice with their money. I frequently say, *there's a reason that doctors practice on cadavers.*

As an expert, your narrow focus will bring you notoriety and financial rewards. Even though this may seem obvious to business veterans, many entrepreneurs and self-employed people have trouble saying "no" to opportunities. Many figure that with some on the job training, they will figure it out. That's a terrible plan. Learn to say no to anything that is not in your sweet spot. Start saying yes to better opportunities and ask for better compensation for doing that. It will more than make up for the deals you pass up.

79. Lock Arms: Union-Style Collective Bargaining

Entrepreneurs are the smartest and the stupidest people in the world. On the smart side, we are more motivated, innovative, and accomplish more than others. On the other side, we don't usually know how to leverage our collective power and consequently, we waste a lot to time, energy, and resources duplicating efforts that already exist—if we could just learn how to cooperate better, we'd be able to fix that. We need to work together and help each other.

It is critical for entrepreneurs to put their heads together. We should lock arms and tackle problems as a group. A new world brings new problems that require new solutions. The community of professional entrepreneurs is filled with thought leaders, innovators, and trailblazers, but we still need more thought, innovation, and leadership. The world continues to get more complex and the choices more diverse. Many of the problems we have are not going to be addressed by a singular focus or perspective. We need to do a better job of cooperating and pay less attention to just talking about it unproductively.

In the last year, I assembled a brilliant group of real estate deal makers to cooperate on building a technology-driven "capital raising engine" that we can all share. By putting the InvestorValet group of deal promoters together, I got an east coast brokerage firm to sponsor us and give our group a compensation structure that will be north of many millions of dollars per year. If I went to the same firm by myself and said, "we would like to hire you," they would have sent me packing because my personal volume was too low for them, but 50+ deal promoters together does very hefty volume in aggregate, and that made the brokerage firm very enthusiastic about working with us.

Suppose you approach a company about sponsoring you and your company. They look at the numbers of hits on your website, and the numbers alone just do not add up to enough people for the company to be interested.

Conversely, imagine if a group of 30 or 50 service providers approached a sponsor and offered a more powerful level of collaboration. Now the collective number of views and hits could be in the millions and this might interest the company to sponsor the individuals as a collective group. Then when you divide up the money (evenly or pro-rata based on numbers of hits), each person will likely receive more than they could have by themselves. And what stops that group from getting many more such sponsorships?

The growth is geometric—not arithmetic. This is because companies have an easier time thinking about bigger numbers, more impact, and bigger bang for the buck. Don't be timid. Think bigger. Deliver more and ask for more. Make a bigger impact as a group and watch the negotiations start going your way.

The problem is that not all providers want to play together nicely in the sandbox (really, that's most people—not just us), but if they want to increase exposure and bargaining power, they have to learn to collaborate for everyone's benefit. And over the course of putting a group together, if you encounter someone who is not a fit for your sandbox, send them to a different playground!

80. Own the Means of Production

Manufacturing companies sometimes own the plant used to produce the merchandise or inventory to provide them with more control, consistency, and speed. Similarly, service providers—if they cooperated—could control the critical inputs in their businesses and share the expenses in a most cost efficient manner. Examples of critical functions include generating leads, managing calendars, and other administrative functions. Everyone could share resources and build their own quasi bureaus, management agencies, marketing firms, SEO shops, and PR firms to generate business opportunities. Of course, if there are companies who are delivering high quality opportunities, then maybe there is no reason to build an alternative to them, but these concepts are not mutually exclusive.

81. Build an Arsenal of F-You Money

Ultimately, the goal of the material in this book is to help you to generate and put aside enough money that you can call your own shots. Building a stash of F-You money will allow you to turn down gigs that you don't want and it will allow you to walk away from people who do not treat you with the respect and dignity that you deserve. It's hard to say "no" when you need the money. Savings don't happen by accident; they only happen with planning. You have to decide how much you are going to put aside and begin creating your nest egg of F-You money today. You need to put yourself in a position of strength so you don't have to prostitute yourself and do things you don't want to do. When you have money, you can walk away. You can say you don't need a gig, and stand your ground. You also have to power to ask for more money. Without F-You money, you will be at the mercy of the almighty dollar, rather than being in control.

82. Look for the Lines

Paul Orfalea, the guy who founded Kinko's (now a company owned by FedEx), used to say that when you see a line, there is a good chance the demand exists to start a business to solve that problem. When you get the same requests over and over, start a business—don't hire yourself out so someone else can collect the big money for solving the problem. When my clients and audience members started asking for my help in getting them access to CrowdFunding capital, I set up www.InvestorValet.com and started selling shares in the company, raising capital from individual partners. Plus, each of their participating company's (each of which is owned by the individual partners) had to pay a license fee to participate in the company—which we call "taking a seat at the table". As the founder (the person who noticed the opportunity and took action on it), I get the majority of the shares that were issued, as well as the lion's share of the fees. So ask yourself where you notice demand. How might that affect your strategy?

83. Prepare the Problem For a Solution

Some people are just so negative that no matter what you suggest, they will find shortcomings with your solution. They are the people who—when someone else makes a suggestion—counter with "the problem is…" Of course, every solution has a hole in it—nothing is perfect or bulletproof. I find the positive way of turning this logic around is by saying, "the problem we have to solve is…" Once you frame the situation like this, you immediately get on the road to being better off than you were before. It works pretty well for me.

84. Stay Philosophically Congruent

There is a phenomenon I have seen in business over and over: clients run full steam for ninety yards, and then do something really stupid at the ten-yard line (there are plenty of professional football teams that also follow this pattern). They make decisions that make perfect sense and produce great results across all but ten percent of the field. They get so close to finishing up with a polished product, but then decide to cut corners, or do something that doesn't really make sense in the long run, and they end up cheating themselves. Don't fall victim to this; you want to stay committed to great results all the way through. You want to make sure that what you are doing, saying, and promoting makes sense throughout everything you produce and present. This is philosophical congruence.

If you're going to charge a premium rate for your services, your experience, presentation, pedigree, appearance, and the value of the message must all be congruent. The whole package has to make sense—every bit of your package must resonate at the most elite level. There are lots of ways to make the package make sense, but here are a few elements your clients might consider when deciding whether to book you for the project:

> Does this vendor have extensive experience with the relevant field and skills? For example, if they want to hire you to train people on how to build a million dollar company, maybe you've sold a multi-million-dollar company that you built from the ground up.

> Does the vendor consistently have a full calendar of clients?

> What is the vendor's overall presence, appearance, and level of brilliance?

If the service provider has holes in their shoes, has little experience, and has done low-fee or even free work, then there might be a congruence problem if he tries to jump to a higher level on the fee ladder. It is important that what you are offering clients makes sense emotionally, intellectually, and philosophically.

A very sharp and talented colleague recently handed me a book to review and then speak with him about building his business around it. I told him I would read it and get back with him in a few days. The editing was so sloppy that the book was unbearable to read. It contained the types of errors that would get you flogged by an eighth grade English teacher. My focus went from reviewing the content to going through the first chapter and circling all of the errors. I could not get past that point.

I got the guy on the phone and said, "This is horrible. You need to pull this book immediately; it is going to kill your business."

He failed to have it properly edited. An entrepreneur spends months writing a book, and then spends no money getting it edited. An editor would say, "Do you really want credibility from this work? Do you want people to think you are smart?" The answer is obviously "Yes."

Then why would you trust only yourself to proofread a book for distribution into the world? "Don't skimp" is the bottom line. Everything matters. No one wants to look stupid. And in this case, poor proofing could make an otherwise sharp guy look bad. Do you see the incongruity?

"Fake it 'til you make it" is not a great strategy. When the message is not philosophically congruent, we might scratch our heads, knowing something is not right, whether we can put our fingers on the disconnect or not. But one thing is for sure: buyers don't buy when the package doesn't make sense or when things are not philosophically congruent.

85. Engage Experts to See What You Cannot

Different people excel at different things. Maybe it's art, engineering, or math. Some people can read foreign languages. Some can read music. Others read x-rays. For me, it's numbers, financial statements, and black-jack tables.

When I review financial statements, I do not see the same things as untrained people. We all see the same numbers, but because of my experience, I see much more. There was a time that I went to the dermatologist and showed her a red blotch on my arm. She said, "this is not a red blotch. It is a 'blah blah blah'" (some medical term that was about 9 syllables long). We looked at the same spot, but saw entirely different things.

It would be naïve to think the doctor and I would see the same thing even though we both looked at the same blotch. The untrained eye cannot read x-rays or medical scans. Just like those of us who are not musically inclined would never even try to bring a sheet of music to life.

Why, then, do untrained people assume they can read or interpret financial reports, audit reports, or tax returns like a highly trained financial professional? I am not criticizing, but rather, expressing concern and spreading caution because when looking at financial reports, there is "gold in them hills," but without some training, you're probably not going to find it. So you have a choice: learn how to read them, or depend on others to read them for you.

86. Prioritize Financial Literacy

All people involved in business should have a minimum level of financial skills, and for that reason, I encourage financial literacy and insist on some training for the people who surround me. All of us should have basic financial training so we can understand and respond to problems and opportunities as they arise. On the boards of directors on which I have sat, I educated our other board members to help them be better stewards of the capital and the organizations that we are charged with overseeing. I hope this will become your priority also.

COMMON SENSE ISN'T ALWAYS COMMON PRACTICE

I always find it interesting that so many of us know the right answer or the right thing to do, but we so frequently take actions that are so different than what we intellectually know is right or smart. It's time to put your common sense into common practice.

87. Let Go of a Million

Do you want a seven-figure business? What a great gimmick. People fall for it every day. A million is a lot, and not everyone is set up to operate at that level; it usually takes a team of people to accomplish. And you must recognize that it requires infrastructure, special skills, and an enormous amount of work. Plus, making a million doesn't mean that you get to take a million home with you. Most revenue has a cost to produce that revenue (called "cost of goods sold"), in addition to the basic overhead of your company.

I recently saw an interesting analysis stating what it takes to make a $1,000,000. The goal of the meme was to get people to see how little it really is and how easy hitting the target should be, but you be the judge on whether accomplishing any of these is easy or hard. Remember, these numbers are gross before expenses—and we almost never get to keep all of what we make.

Scenario 1
5,000 people to buy a $200 product
2,000 people to buy a $500 product
1,000 people to buy a $1000 product
500 people to buy a $2,000 product
300 people to buy a $3,333 product

Alternatively, Scenario 2
5,000 people to pay $17 per month for 12 months
2,000 people to pay $42 per month for 12 months
1,000 people to pay $83 per month for 12 months
500 people to pay $167 per month for a 12 months
300 people to pay $278 per month for 12 months

For most people, $1,000,000 is an astronomical number, so choose a number that is high, but obtainable (it doesn't even have to have seven figures). If you are not an enterprise operation with employees and other overhead, wouldn't $900,000 be pretty good? Just sayin'.

88. Don't Make Money Complicated

Money does not have to be complicated, so don't make it complicated. One of my partners was reviewing our fund documents and he could not calculate the profit-sharing number. His number did not match mine. He boastfully told me that he was trained as an engineer, and as such, he had taken every advanced course in mathematics offered at the university level. I politely told him that as a CPA, I had taken every arithmetic class offered at the elementary school level. Needless to say, in 3 minutes, I showed him how he had over-complicated the formula. Use the decades-old KISS formula: Keep it Simple, Stupid!

89. Avoiding Getting Your Brain Picked

As consultants, advisors, and service professionals who deal in intellectual property, the worst outcome is one where someone picks your brain for free. But there is a formula that I have developed to give out just enough information so you don't feel bad and the prospect starts begging for more—for a fee!

People invite me for coffee all the time because they want to pick my brain about something or another. If those people are business prospects, I usually politely decline. If they buy a ticket to my symposium—which is a great first step for someone who wants to be in my business, network, and world to demonstrate they are serious, committed to doing some business, and have some skin in the game—then I most always go for that cup of coffee.

And then I share openly. I answer all of their questions and help them figure out if running a fund like I do is a good fit for them. I don't work on the clock. I am focused on helping them address the issues on their minds— knowing that much more business could be on the horizon, depending on whether they want to move forward. But I never talk someone into it. Moving forward is a personal decision, and my batting average for success is always more important than any fees I might receive for helping to set up companies, funds, or business structures.

But for everyone else, only give away the "what" for free. If we are not being paid, we can tell people "what" to do. But we must charge for the "how". When prospects ask "how" to do whatever you told them to do, advise them that the answer is part of the consulting assignment that will be covered by your engagement fee.

90. Opt For Advertising Over Commission

Advertising is the least expensive form of marketing on a per-unit basis. This may seem counter-intuitive, but think about it. Small companies and entrepreneurs like to pay their salespeople based on commission because they have frequently have no money—or at least not enough money to pay salaries or fund other compensation strategies. But if you had plenty of money, how would you pay? Is the commission-only salesperson aligned with your goals, timing, and priorities? Is paying sizable commissions the most cost-effective approach? Probably not which is why you would prefer people whom you pay to be dedicated to you. Think about the differences between freelancers, agents, and dedicated salespeople. Who is completely dedicated to your success, who is partially dedicated to it, and who is the least concerned with it? As a business owner, you want to stack your deck with talented resources that advocate for you as much and as often as possible.

Consider the most plentiful source of low-priced labor: interns. They will usually work for free (watch out for local labor laws here), but is the best solution for you truly a "free" (or very low cost) resource? More often than not, you are not the intern's highest priority. They may have classes, exams, part-time paying jobs, or other volunteer work, which can potentially interfere with your requirements. Isn't having an employee's full and undivided attention mandatory—or at least preferable?

Even still, in the early stages of a business, it may make sense for you to be someone's secondary priority or to pay someone a rather high percentage sales commission on a success-fee basis, if you don't have the funds to hire them outright. But as you grow, the commission-only structure should morph into a base plus commission arrangement, which could eventually diminish until there is no commission paid at all.

Frequently, larger companies avoid commissions altogether in favor of using vehicles with greater reach, such as television and print advertisements, as these methods are mere pennies per person you reach. And ironically, on a percentage of the total sale, traditional media tools are a mere fraction of what commissions cost. And of course, in between mass media and straight, commission-only salespeople, digital and targeted tools are the tools of choice as marketing budgets begin to grow.

Don't misunderstand. I like paying people for being successful. And I like commissions. I want the best people to be rewarded. I am just concerned with making sure that you structure your business affairs in a way that gives you the best odds for success. So think carefully. The cheapest choice is not always the best choice.

91. Get Paid For Thinking

Overall, self-employed people don't do a great job of billing for their time. We tend to focus on the fee rather than what that fee represents in work hours because frequently, the hours required to do the job are not known in advance when the agreements are being set up.

Your value and experience go beyond what you deliver to the client. Your time and the time you commit to solving problems may have an even greater value than your fee. It is all about how you leverage and monetize your time. Sometimes—although you have seen a problem many times—the particular solution requires great thought and consideration. It might require such intense thought that billing on an hourly basis is not a reasonable way to bill for solving the problem—especially if you come up with the solution pretty quickly.

A past client had terrible financial problems. They brought me in to rethink their strategy, refocus their efforts, and help them attract some capital—and they knew from the people who referred me into the company that I was the right resource to help bring solutions to the table. After sharing the issues, the company asked for my plan and the fee. When I said I would think about their problems for "a six figure sum" and then get back to them with a plan, it was no surprise that they pushed back—and they were pretty arrogant in their refusal. So I also responded arrogantly, telling them, "I'm not the one with problems." That was cocky—more than I generally like to be - but this company was broken, and there was no bigger sledgehammer than a big number to think about how to fix their sorry situation. They reluctantly agreed, but when I came back six weeks later with a solution and plan for the problem the board of directors loved, I was awarded a multi-year contract, plus a very material percentage of ownership in the company—in addition to what they had already paid me.

The moral of the story: be bold. If you know you have the goods, and as long as you aren't fooling around, put your hand out far and make "the ask". Notice there are several of my concepts working here: money follows expertise, yield, congruence, and understanding the client's pain, to name a few.

If prospects see you as someone who has the expertise and the experience to make a huge difference in their business, go ahead and ask them to pay you a fee to "think" through a problem and then come through with the solution. You have to deliver big, so the payoff should be big for both the client and for you.

You have to have some real competency and confidence in those skills, but when you come through with the deliverable, you have created a new business model for yourself. Thinking, strategizing, and high-level advisory services is a viable business model that I recommend some entrepreneurs adopt—and taking payment for the strategic thinking in both cash and stock are models that could also work for many experienced advisors.

SHOW ME THE MONEY

At the end of the day, it always seems like business is about money, but it's not. Business is about people, and if you take care of the people around you in just the right ways, they will help you to make all the money you want.

92. Pay Yourself Off the Top and Bottom
Paying "off the top" and "off the bottom" means getting paid for both your time and the value you add. Calculate payments due to you off the top and off the bottom.

This idea is especially relevant when working with a partner (or partners). Suppose you partner with someone to write a book. They are doing most of the writing, so they get paid $1000 off the top for the writing work. The book is completed and then you both agree to a 50/50 split of the profits, and the book makes $10,000. You subtract the $1,000 payment to the writer and then cut the remaining $9,000 in half so you each receive $4,500. Now your writing partner was paid $5,500 to your $4,500. Note that the sharing percentages do not all have to be equal either so 1/3 – 2/3 can work also. But people should be paid for what they do - off the top (called gross revenue) and the agreed on split off the bottom (which is called net profit).

93. Pay People for Exactly What They Do
Compensation strategies hugely affect your success. This applies to how you pay others, as well as how you negotiate the compensation you receive.

Always pay people for what they do. That means you might pay for multiple activities. For example, I might pay a writer for writing, but if the same person is capable of doing layout work, I would pay for that separately. Some people will suggest that it's just easier to make a bulk payment for everything—but "everything" gets clumsy, so it is better to treat each component individually—though you can eventually write one check for everything. It helps to create better long-term relationships, it avoids misunderstandings, and it helps you to determine who the best people are to do the jobs you need done. If you are going to break out the fees for each service, you can make the best and most informed decision about who to hire and what to pay.

94. Bet on What You Control

Everybody wants us to work for free or they want to pay on performance. Performance deals are great—if you do them right. I like those deals—as long as I have some control over the outcome.

If I am asked to work "on the come" (in other words betting on a future outcome) in whole or in part, I will usually double the part that is risk-based. I think carefully about opportunities that have a component of risk. Who controls the risk? If I control it, then I will always take the risk—but if someone else (like the client) controls the risk, then I will rarely accept the risk because it is more of a gamble than a calculated decision. Be extra careful with risks that you do not control. For example, if a client asks you to take x% of the savings you (or your ideas) create or of the revenue you (or your ideas) generate, beware. Who is creating the improvement? Who is calculating it? If the client is doing all of the work, take a large percentage because you have little control over the outcome and you are likely to get only a small amount of what you believe you should receive. If you control the outcome, you can take a smaller amount because you do not have to police the books and records with the same level of scrutiny, and because there is probably a higher certainty of a payout.

Suppose I am working as a consultant for a company. I want to get paid for my time and work (off the top), but I may also want some participation off the bottom (based on the results I helped to create). I have to be reasonable in what I ask for percentage-wise and I must be a direct participant of the implementation of the ideas I bring to the table. It is not going to be good enough to just do a workshop and put forth some ideas; I must be in the trenches to make sure that concepts are implemented and that there is a measurable outcome of which I can have a percentage.

95. Put Your Affairs in Order

If you're someone who doesn't have their financial affairs in order—either because your debts are too big or because your retirement is underfunded—get over being embarrassed about it, organize a group of people to work on these issues with you, and make these problems go away. If all self-employed entrepreneurs were able to take better care of themselves, many industries would be better off. By working together and being less embarrassed now and more proud later, we can help each other be better off, make more money, and accomplish the things that we really want to so that we can all be self-sufficient.

Wealth is all about getting the money to work for you. You might be a high-income earner or even a medium-income earner, but if you don't have money working for you, you're never wealthy in the true economic sense of the word.

Put simply, what wealth buys you is freedom, peace of mind, the opportunity to enjoy your life more, and the opportunity to do the things that you want to. Hopefully, it does not turn you into someone who is boastful, egotistical, or unfriendly. And hopefully, once you start making a great amount of money, you won't post pictures on Facebook that serve no other purpose than to show off or make other people feel bad.

When you make money and are saving for your family's future, it is imperative to be hyper-responsible with their money. The single biggest step my wife and I took for our own personal planning (besides life insurance on me years ago) was the development and creation of an estate plan. All adults in this country have an estate plan. The question is whether it is the plan you created for yourself or it's the default plan the government has for you. Our estate attorney, Steven M. Greenwood advises, "woe to you if you end up on the government plan—and in probate". Work with a qualified estate-planning attorney in your state to take care of this right away. Not only will you sleep better at night, but you will stand tall knowing you have done all you can do to protect your family.

96. Get Out of Consumer Debt

Eliminate consumer debt by paying down the highest interest rate money first—not based on the size of the balance or the quantity of credit lines. This saves you bigger money in the long run. One by one, pay them off.

Try to settle out of tougher debt. If you are behind in any debts, consider not paying any further and settle instead. The bigger the debt, the more power you have. You can negotiate with the banks and lenders. They want money, and to them, *some* money is better than no money and a charge off. You may not have the skills to look at your financial situation, so find someone who can help you. You will not randomly get yourself out of the hole. You may need help, so go and get it. Negotiating and settling debts is a skill, and it's probably best not to practice on yourself.

Once you begin working to get out of bad situation, get into the habit of monitoring your credit report. Clean it up and make sure the lines of credit you pay off are noted on your report. Monitoring your credit reports is also the first line of defense against someone stealing your identity.

You should also consider engaging a credit clean up service to remove the blemishes on your credit report. The credit reporting system in the United States is very unfavorable to entrepreneurs and self-employed people because we carry more debt and we tend to have more entries on our reports than our corporate counter-parts for whom the system was designed. That means that blemishes hurt us worse. I see the system as a game, except no one ever tells us the rules about how the scores are calculated, so do not delay. Learn to play the game and get this part of your life under control as fast as you can.

THE BIG KAHUNA – MONEY OUT OF THIN AIR

On Wall Street, money seems to come out of thin air and since a comprehensive description of how that happens would be encyclopedic, it is outside of the scope of this book. Just know that the thousands of dot-com millionaires indeed got their money out of thin air, and I am quite certain they don't work any harder than the rest of us do, but because they owned company stock, and the stock price went up, they made a lot—out of thin air. The lesson is: own things, because it's really hard to make a lot working on the clock.

97. Get Stable, Lower Costs

Actually, as you get better at your craft and as your volume goes up, many of your costs should come down, but the one that is least obvious is the cost of your money. The better you are and the more stable your business is, the lower your risk profile should be. If you are borrowing money—say as an advance against upcoming work or for capital needed to fulfill a contract—the better you become and the lower your risk, and the less it should cost you in interest for certain types of loans.

98. Find Out Where the Money Really Is

This is counter-intuitive for people who want to get better at their craft, but it's the truth: the money is usually not in the craft. The money is in the money. If you think the money is in your skills, you are leaving money on the table. The money is always somewhere else, and you need to look for it– it might really be in consulting and advising. That's the reason for strategic planning and the creating of business models. The exercises needed to create these plans force us to think through the issues and answer questions such as, "where is the big money going to come from"?

99. Get in on the Big Money

For investors, the big money is always made in the private placement phase; you need to get into early stage companies early. There is a misconception that "going public" is where the money is, but that's not so. Facebook went public at $45 per share and four years later, it is roughly triple the price, so an investor would have made about 200%. Pretty good. But imagine buying the shares at a penny, nickel or dime each. The percentages are staggering. What going public does is unlocks the equity so the shareholder can convert those shares into cash. That's why the media says after an Initial Public Offering (IPO), "xyz person became a billionaire today"—because what was only on paper during the private placement phase becomes real when the shares can be sold on the public market. The truth is, they were a billionaire the day before, but after the IPO, they could sell their shares and take the cash so they could place it somewhere else.

The JOBS Act of 2012 loosened the laws of private securities. It has allowed entrepreneurs more access to funds. Now if your neighbor has the next home run idea, any of us can invest in that idea if the entrepreneur wants to raise some capital by issuing private securities. We may assemble some of those great ideas on www.TheNextHomeRun.com at some point in the future.

100. Get Close to the Money

You make more money the closer you get to the money. This is why school teachers make the least and traders on Wall Street make the most. I'm not saying it's fair, but it is how it is. Departments that make money or move money probably have more money to spend and find it easier to measure their returns on expenditures and capital outlays. It is why sales departments have bigger budgets than departments that are considered overhead.

If making money matters to you, get close to the money. Seek out companies that have money, and clients that have money. Work with the departments that bring in the money or control the money. Consider your target audience—if they are individuals, do they get close to making the money you want to make? If they are all broke or working for hourly wage, they are not close to the money.

101. Make Your Fans Your Funders
The ultimate goal in customer service and client relationships used to be to create fans. But now, we can take these fans to the next level and create shareholder relationships with them using the new investment crowdfunding rules. Imagine having hundreds of people, each with a tiny financial interest in your success?

The money you need to start any business or endeavor is located right inside your "fanbase". Cultivate it and let it work for you. Raising money for a real business (not a lifestyle one) is a very reasonable goal. Who would pony up? Your fans! So this isn't too hard. Though investment crowdfunding is new, be on the lookout for opportunities to take advantage of it. This is the next BIG thing!

102. Take Your Assets Public - the New Personal IPO
The new law for investors under the JOBS Act of 2012 details the investment crowdfunding rules, which make it possible for entrepreneurs with asset-rich libraries and large fan bases to take these assets public in ways that were previously only available to the largest companies or wealthiest venture funded companies. All investors are now allowed to participate in the private securities market using the legal paradigm of Investment Crowdfunding.

Investing is no longer reserved for the super-rich. Regular people can invest smaller amounts than they could before without the headaches that had made it so restrictive—compounded by tight regulation from the government. Under the old rules, only millionaires could play. Now new IPOs are being formed. Different kinds of companies are going public. This is an exciting new world with many new places to invest with new ways to raise capital. This is an exploding sector. Keep an eye on it.

103. Raise Capital the Wall Street Way

Some entrepreneurs get to the level where they are making mid- to high-six-figure incomes. The problem many of them face, however, is that they are working themselves into an early grave. They want out, and they have an idea for a business to get them out, but they don't know how to go about getting capital to start it up.

Some believe they need venture capital. This is "Shark Tank" money. I live in that tank; people pitch me deals and I have a fund I can use to buy in. What people do not realize is that the world of venture capitalists is vicious. If you fall down and scrape your knee, the investor can quickly take over your company. This is not for beginners, nor for the faint of heart.

Venture capitalists are not interested in companies in the start-up or testing phase. They only deal with companies that are in their growth stage with explosive potential and likelihood for a future IPO so they can pull their money out.

If you need money early on to get your business started, seek out angel investors, like friends and family. There are many sites that allow you to ask for capital. Once you grow your business, *then* you can consider creating a business structure in which people can buy shares. This is private securities, which is different than public securities like buying shares of Apple. If you need this type of capital, make sure a securities attorney is supervising your every move. And remember, securities attorneys are not the garden-variety attorneys you find in the yellow pages. These are highly specialized people whose job it is to keep you out of prison for violating some of the strictest rules in the country.

FINAL THOUGHTS

Now that I've shared over a hundred insights, tips, and tricks with you, I hope you feel ready to make some changes in your business. In order to control your outcomes, you have to have control of the inputs—and that encompasses every part of your life, your business, and plans. The opportunities are out there and they are endless, but you have to go and get them. I know you can do this! And now, as my parting gifts to you, I leave you with some final inspiration!

104. Own the Gate: Produce Your Own Programs

Entrepreneurs make a lot of noise about how much our fees are and about how busy we are. My goal is not to be busy. It is to be productive. And on the subject of fees, no one values my time or services as highly as I do. No one pays on the schedule that I want like I do.

People are funny. We all like to get our way—and none of us gets our way all the time. We all have a way of dealing with "not getting our way" that comes from when we were small children. Some take a downward turn at the end of the road—they fold up the tent and go home. Some people are motivated to try even harder and bang on even more doors after being turned down—sometimes to the point of near insanity (remember, the definition of insanity is doing the same thing over and over again expecting a different result). And some people learn from the school of hard knocks that they have to go back to the drawing board and somehow reinvent. I am one of those whose determination goes up with every "no"

I receive. Tell me I can't do something, and I will explode with energy, enthusiasm, and focus on the "impossible accomplishment".

When I wanted to get into the speaking business, and I couldn't get bureaus to hire me and I didn't know how to get business organizations to engage me (which I thought would be a slam dunk given my business background), I did the only thing I knew how to do: I started my own seminar company, retaining ownership of the gate and hiring salespeople to fill up the room with people who would pay to listen to me. This is my pattern. I own almost everything I hope to get business benefit from. It's how I think. I hope you will start to think at least a little bit, like this too.

Of course I don't have the money to do everything I want (nobody does), so sometimes I have to get the money from other people—but that is an advanced topic for another time. Just know that in the United States of America, you can own almost anything and everything you want.

105. Engage Your Heart

We've all been up and we've all been down. If you run across people who are down, go easy on them. Treat them the way you would like to be treated. It's good business and it's good humanity. Doing good will come back around and reward you multi-fold. Get involved in your community. Join a non-profit board of directors. The networking is different than what you probably do now—there tend to be lots of corporate types on these boards.

When I was down on my luck, many of my supposed friends disappeared. There were plenty of friends when I was successful. Don't be a fair-weather friend. You don't have to be an ass to be successful. There are plenty decent human beings who are successful. Lend a hand when you can. We can do a lot for each other.

The deal with networking is that you have to give to get. Sometimes this means giving a bit of your expertise, but when it comes down to doing work, you need to charge. Good deeds are not forgotten, however, and often when we help someone, in the future, they may pay you back—or at least just be there for you.

106. Be the TV Show for Somebody's Commercial

I recently had a friend from the pharmaceutical business talk to me about the difficulties he was having generating leads. I suggested that he invite 20 or so doctors and do a presentation for them.

"They won't sit through a commercial about my business," he replied.

I suggested that we co-sponsor an event because his contacts would be good leads for me too. I would come in and do a presentation on Hedge Funds for the doctors; he would then be the commercial at the end. I would introduce him as the sponsor of the event and he could talk about what he does after the doctors got a powerful, eye-opening investment discussion. It was a brilliant plan, and we set up a program to present to 75 doctors to over a three-day period in Louisiana.

This was beneficial to me because I was able to use the leads from my presentation for my business, and it would not cost thousands of dollars from my marketing budget because he was setting it up. I also saved on labor and administration so it was a true win-win.

107. Don't Quit Your Day Job—Yet

If you are not yet a well-paid entrepreneur, here is the best advice I can give you:

If you want to be fantastically successful in your business, don't count on the money when you are getting started. Have a different primary source of revenue and layer your business' income on top of that. Plowback—or parlay—the earnings into the new business so you are well set up for success.

Running your own business is much tougher than it looks, so don't quit your day job until this one starts to pan out. Transition into your business and don't let go of your other revenue-producing activities until your business revenue heats up.

All of us who are successful in business have seen a lot of corpses lying by the side of the road. It's best not to have that destiny in your future. Even advanced entrepreneurs could do a better job of plowing some earnings back into their businesses. Reinvest in your business and in yourself. It will pay off big time.

FINALLY

Armed with the knowledge from this book, I want you to think hard about your business. Ask questions, partner with others, solve problems, and plan for the future. There are probably more fun tasks or projects on your plate but none are much more important.

Work with others who can check their egos at the door and cooperate for the common good. We are not competitors. We have to work together to continue to improve and elevate our collective skills—both on the platform and in business. Plus, we need to continue to be creative, always generating and sharing great ideas.

To learn more about How to Stop Hustling Gigs and Start Building a Business, go to:
www.StopHustlingGigs.com

ABOUT THE AUTHOR

Joel G. Block
Chief Deal Maker
Bullseye Capital
5737 Kanan Road, Suite 269
Agoura Hills, CA 91301

Office: (818) 597-2990
Fax: (818) 337-7537
joel@bullseyecap.com
www.bullseyecap.com
Twitter: @joelblock

Licenses:

❯ Certified Public Accountant, Active in California, (License #: 118277). First issued in 1988.

❯ Real Estate Broker, CA Department of Real Estate; (License #: 00896489). First Issued 1987

❯ Life and Health - California Department of Insurance; Licensed since 2002. (License #: 0D50987)..

Degree:

❯ B.S. Accounting, Major

❯ Real Estate Finance Minor.

Joel is a real world, 25+ year veteran of the venture capital, private equity and Hedge Fund world who addresses audiences from Silicon Valley venture firms to Wall Street bankers on matters of capital formation and most recently, on Investment CrowdFunding. Twice each year, Joel hosts and headlines the standard-setting Real Estate Syndication and Hedge Fund Symposium program, educating and advising CPAs, attorneys, investment bankers and asset class specialists on organizing and running investment pools.

He is a professional investor who has been a principal in over 30 syndicated real estate and entrepreneurial transactions in addition to advising on dozens more. Joel is CEO of the Bullseye Capital Fund and founder of the National Association of Syndicators. Joel has taught thousands of real estate brokers, CPAs, attorneys, and Investors about raising capital and best practices for structuring group investments. Joel is a nationally recognized expert in Private Placements, Reg D Offerings, Operating Agreements, deal structure, valuations, tax issues and capital raising approaches with both accredited and non-accredited Investors.

A professional speaker, Joel is a persuasive and engaging communicator. He naturally demystifies complex issues and forensics for laymen. As a leader, Joel is humble, likable, friendly, and easy to relate to and was the foreman of a successful jury. His work has appeared in the *Los Angeles Times, Wall Street Journal, Forbes Small Business, Entrepreneur Magazine, Investor's Business Daily*, and the *Los Angeles Business Journal*. Joel is a professional member of the National Speakers Association, where he holds the prestigious Certified Speaking Professional designation plus he is a member of the elite NSA Million Dollar Speakers Group. And though he doesn't admit often, Joel is also a CPA.

Additional Reference Materials

Expert Witness
http://tinyurl.com/help-attorneys

LinkedIn
http://www.linkedin.com/in/joelblock

Wikipedia
http://en.wikipedia.org/wiki/Joel_G._Block

Bullseye Capital Hedge Fund
http://www.bullseyecapfund.com

NOTES

NOTES

NOTES

NOTES

Made in the USA
San Bernardino, CA
22 November 2017